ARTIFICIAL INTELLIGENCE

BUILDING SMARTER MACHINES

STEPHANIE SAMMARTINO McPHERSON

TWENTY-FIRST CENTURY BOOKS / MINNEAPOLIS

For my husband, Richard

The author and publisher wish to thank Dr. Maria Gini, CSE Distinguished Professor of Computer Science and Engineering at the University of Minnesota, for her assistance with this manuscript. The author also thanks Peg Goldstein and Domenica Di Piazza for expert editorial guidance and support and Richard McPherson for encouragement and help.

Twenty-First Century Books
A division of Lerner Publishing Group, Inc.
241 First Avenue North
Minneapolis, MN 55401 USA

For reading levels and more information, look up this title at www.lernerbooks.com.

Main body text set in Adobe Garamond Pro 11/15.
Typeface provided by Adobe Systems.

Library of Congress Cataloging-in-Publication Data

Names: McPherson, Stephanie Sammartino, author.
Title: Artificial intelligence : building smarter machines / by Stephanie Sammartino McPherson.
Description: Minneapolis : Twenty-First Century Books, [2017] | Audience: Ages 13–18. | Audience: Grades 9–12. | Includes bibliographical references and index.
Identifiers: LCCN 2016034037 (print) | LCCN 2016051146 (ebook) | ISBN 9781512418262 (lb : alk. paper) | ISBN 9781512448627 (eb pdf)
Subjects: LCSH: Artificial intelligence—Juvenile literature. | Artificial intelligence—History—Juvenile literature. | Artificial intelligence—Technological innovations—Juvenile literature. | Conscious automata—Juvenile literature. | Robots—Control—Juvenile literature.
Classification: LCC Q335.4 .M387 2017 (print) | LCC Q335.4 (ebook) | DDC 006.3—dc23

LC record available at https://lccn.loc.gov/2016034037

Manufactured in the United States of America
1-41166-23176-2/27/2017

CONTENTS

CHAPTER 1

DAWN OF A NEW AGE

The popular television program *Jeopardy!* had never generated so much excitement. The date was February 11, 2011. Ken Jennings and Brad Rutter, the two top winners in the game show's twenty-seven-year history, had returned to vie for a $1 million prize. But the real star of the show, the reason for all the anticipation, was the third contestant. Watson was a "smart machine," an artificial intelligence (AI) developed over four years by twenty-five computer engineers at the technology corporation IBM. The engineers had designed Watson specifically to challenge *Jeopardy!* champions.

Artificial intelligence, machinery with the ability to reason and solve problems, was nothing new. For decades, scientists had been trying, with limited success, to instill basic human skills, such as understanding language and recognizing objects, into machines. *Jeopardy!* posed especially formidable challenges.

A game show with a twist, *Jeopardy!* reverses the normal question-and-answer format. Instead of asking questions, show host Alex Trebek gives answers, called clues, and contestants provide the questions. For example, if Trebek says, "the author of *Harry Potter*," the contestant who hits a buzzer first replies, "Who is J. K. Rowling?"

Watson had to comprehend the full meaning of each clue to succeed at *Jeopardy!* Was the phrasing straightforward or tricky? Did it involve word play or humor? Watson would require a huge knowledge base to cover the broad range of categories—everything

Ken Jennings *(left)* and Brad Rutter *(right)* compete with Watson *(center)*, an artificial intelligence created by IBM, during a practice round on the TV quiz show *Jeopardy!* In the final contest, Watson beat out the two humans to win a $1 million prize.

from sports to science to popular culture—that show up on *Jeopardy!* To prepare for the show, computer scientists downloaded vast amounts of information from the Internet to give Watson the huge number of facts that it needed. "Just like any other contestant, Watson has been studying up," said a member of the Watson team before the contest.

As the cameras rolled for the *Jeopardy!* broadcast, Watson seemed to stand right there between its competitors. But its television presence, a logo on a computer screen, was just for show. The real Watson, comprising ten racks of computer servers, was located off-site. Instead of listening to the statements read by Trebek, Watson received its clues as digital text that it analyzed at lightning speed. Its performance wasn't perfect, but it quickly established a lead over its human opponents. By the end of the third day, it had won the $1 million purse.

Ken Jennings, famous for his seventy-four-game winning streak on the show, took his defeat in stride. "I for one welcome our new computer overlords," he said.

For those who fear that machines really could come to dominate humans, Jennings's statement hit close to home. Watson's victory raises difficult questions. Did Watson really think? Did it understand its participation in a quiz show? Can machines acquire self-awareness? If so, is this a promising or a dangerous situation for humans?

Scientists and technologists have come down on both sides of the debate. Some, such as computer scientist Raymond Kurzweil, director of engineering at Google, predict that artificial intelligence will improve life for all humanity and may even extend the human life span indefinitely. Others, such as British physicist Stephen Hawking, fear that the age of supersmart machines could threaten our very existence on Earth. Although no machine, not even Watson, comes close to matching human intelligence, many scientists believe it is only a matter of time before technology reaches this milestone.

STRONG AND WEAK

Experts on artificial intelligence divide the machines into several types. An artificial general intelligence (AGI), also called a strong artificial intelligence, would be a true thinking machine, able to learn on its own and modify its own programming without human input. In theory, an AGI would be able to solve any problem that a human could decipher.

DEEP BLUE

Jeopardy! was not the first game in which humans faced a machine challenger. In the late twentieth century, various organizations staged chess competitions pitting human players against computers, with the humans always coming out on top. A much-publicized six-game match between IBM's Deep Blue computer and Russian world chess champion Garry Kasparov in 1996 also ended with a human victory.

After Deep Blue's defeat, IBM scientists began improving the computer for a rematch the next year. Although the updated computer could review two hundred million possible chess moves each second and choose the ones most likely to lead to victory, Kasparov won the first game. Deep Blue took the second game, but games 3, 4, and 5 ended in draws. Tension mounted as the final game began on May 11, 1997. When Deep Blue won the game, thereby winning the match two games to one, the entire world took note. For many, the victory highlighted in a surprising and vivid way the growing power of computers.

It would not be narrowly tailored to perform a specific task, such as analyzing the stock market or conducting computer searches. Instead, it would be able to deal with a broad range of issues. Over time, as it accumulated knowledge, an AGI would get smarter and smarter.

What worries many experts (and excites others) is the possibility that an AGI might keep improving until it morphed into a super intelligence. Such an entity would far surpass human intellectual abilities. But it might not share human social and ethical values—such as notions of fairness, justice, and right and wrong. Without exceptionally careful programming and built-in safeguards, a supersmart machine could become uncontrollable. An example would be an intelligent robot-weapon capable of selecting and firing on targets in wartime without

human oversight. "We can imagine such technology outsmarting financial markets [human stock traders], out-inventing human researchers, out-manipulating human leaders, and developing weapons we cannot even understand," wrote Stephen Hawking with other concerned scientists in 2014. If, on the other hand, a superintelligence could be programmed to share human goals, the result could help humanity. Such a machine might be able to devise remedies for air and water pollution, climate change caused by the burning of fossil fuels, and life-threatening illnesses.

No such promise or peril looms over the development of weak artificial intelligence, a phenomenon that is already at work in our homes, cars, and workplaces. In contrast to artificial general intelligence, weak AI focuses on specific tasks. Weak AI is currently transforming such diverse fields as transportation, medicine, and banking. Apple's digital virtual assistant Siri operates through weak AI. So do unmanned land rovers that explore and photograph the surface of Mars. Other examples include apps and programs that conduct Internet searches, identify faces and objects in photographs, and translate text and spoken words into foreign languages. Self-driving cars, refrigerators that regulate temperature and monitor food quality, and "smart houses" that track household lighting, temperature, fire safety, and home security are also examples of weak artificial intelligence.

Weak AI has already displaced large numbers of laborers in the workforce. In modern factories, robots (machines that automatically perform complicated and repetitive tasks) handle much of the assembly work—work previously performed by humans. Automatic teller machines, online banking and bill paying, and scanning software do much of the work that bank clerks and tellers used to do. Self-checkout stands at supermarkets have replaced many human cashiers. The replacement of human workers by machines will only accelerate as technology improves. Many analysts fear that millions of workers will be left jobless, as fewer and fewer tasks will require humans to perform them.

INTELLIGENCE TESTS

Can machines think? British computer pioneer and mathematician Alan Turing *(right)* was already considering this question as early as 1950. He devised what came to be called the Turing test to determine a machine's intelligence. The procedure is simple. A person in isolation poses questions and receives answers from both another human being and a computer. If the questioner can't determine which answers come from the human and which come from the computer, a judge can assume that the machine is intelligent. Turing believed that by the year 2000, with advances in AI, computers would fool judges at least 30 percent of the time.

To pass the Turing test, an artificial intelligence must give answers that lead the questioner to believe that he or she is interacting with a human. British computer pioneer and mathematician Alan Turing devised the test in 1950.

Some researchers say that the Turing test has serious flaws. Even though a computer may engage in a seemingly normal conversation, they argue, we can't assume that it is actually thinking. They say that other tests are better able to assess computer intelligence. One such test is the Winograd Schema Challenge. Devised by Hector Levesque of the University of Toronto in 2011, the test presents questions that require reasoning skills. A sample question might be, what is meant by the sentence "The trophy would not fit into the brown suitcase because it was too small"? A person would have no trouble explaining that the suitcase was too small for the trophy. But a computer might have trouble deciphering whether the pronoun *it* refers to the trophy or the suitcase. So more than language analysis is needed to make the determination. Common sense is also required.

In other tests, computers watch programs on television or YouTube and then answer questions about them. For instance, a computer might view a news program and then be asked, why does the congressperson think we need a new law? After watching a sitcom, the computer might have to explain why a particular joke was funny. Experts say that these kinds of tests are much better than the Turing test in assessing a computer's ability to think, reason, and analyze information.

COMPUTERS WITH LEGS AND WINGS

For years, artificial intelligence has been quietly developing behind the scenes. But recent advances in weak AI and robotics are bringing it more and more into the public eye. To some, the term *robots* conjures up images of shiny, metal figures lumbering stiffly around a room. The reality is far more diverse. Robots come in all shapes, sizes, and materials. Some look like humans or animals, while others have no resemblance to living things. Their styles range from the cute to the awesome to the seriously menacing.

It isn't hard to guess what the robot BigDog (developed by the company Boston Dynamics, now owned by Google) is made to resemble. With four legs, a computer to control it, sensors to explore its environment, and an engine to power it, BigDog was designed to carry heavy equipment for

In a rescue drill undertaken by the Russian Emergencies Ministry in 2016, a drone drops a life vest to a struggling swimmer. Rescue agencies use drones and robots in a variety of emergency situations—especially when conditions might be perilous for human responders.

soldiers. Weighing a hefty 240 pounds (109 kilograms) and standing 3 feet (0.9 meters) high, BigDog can run 4 miles (6.4 kilometers) per hour, climb stairs, carry 340-pound (154 kg) loads, and push forward through water, mud, and snow.

In contrast to BigDog, some robots are tiny and delicate. Patterned after insects, they have wings and can fly. The robots function like drones (remotely controlled, unmanned aerial vehicles). They can infiltrate the rubble of collapsed buildings, using sensors to identify carbon dioxide from a survivor's breath or the warmth generated by a living body. Instantly, the robots can radio the person's location to rescue squads. Designers imagine swarms of these insect-like robots released into the ruins of a city after a major earthquake. They would save workers precious minutes or hours in the race to free survivors from a wreckage.

In the performance of their carefully defined duties, BigDog and the swarms of flying rescue robots might almost seem to be aware of what they are doing. But they are not. Complicated algorithms (sets of mathematical rules) programmed into their software guide their actions.

ANDROID DICK

Even more impressive than running and flying robots are robots that are programmed to converse with humans. For example, Android Dick. (An android is a robot that takes a human form.) US sculptor and roboticist David Hanson created the robot to look like the famous US science fiction writer Philip K. Dick, who died in 1982. Hanson uploaded Dick's novels, stories, and conversations with reporters and other writers into the robot's software. Supplied with this data, the robot easily replied to questions the real Dick had answered when he was alive. By analyzing combinations of sounds and words and matching them with meanings from its database, the robot could frame responses to other questions as well. Some of its statements were so convincing that in 2013, a reporter from the TV series *Nova* asked Android Dick the most basic question of all: Was it really able to think?

A Russian television reporter interviews Android Dick at the robot's debut at the NextFest technology exhibition in Chicago in 2005. Programmed with information from the late science fiction author Philip K. Dick's books and other writings, the android can convincingly carry on conversations. It gives answers and observations like those the real Dick might have given when he was alive.

"The best way I can respond to that is to say that everything humans, animals, and robots do is programmed to a degree," replied the android. "As technology improves, it is anticipated that I will be able to integrate new words that I hear online and in real time. I may not get everything right, say the wrong thing, and sometimes may not know what to say, but everyday I make progress. Pretty remarkable, huh?"

AN ALIEN INTELLIGENCE?

Some experts doubt that machines will ever replicate all the complex processes that go on in the human brain. This does not mean that machines will lack intelligence—only that they will have an alien, or different, type of intelligence. Although a machine may sort through thousands of documents in nanoseconds, accomplish multiple tasks simultaneously, and solve problems that would stump the smartest human, it may not be able to experience love or appreciate a sunset. It may be able to analyze what makes a joke funny, use an algorithm to construct its own joke, and even emit a synthetic chuckle. But would the machine experience the delight that humor brings to humans? Would it be able to express and understand courage, honor, or compassion?

Questions abound. Is it possible to program AI with a sense of right and wrong? Will sentient (aware, thinking, and feeling) machines be part of our future? Can artificial intelligence be used to solve the world's pressing problems and make life better for everyone? Was Ken Jennings correctly predicting the future when he called computers "our overlords"? Entertainment though it was, Watson's *Jeopardy!* appearance brought the issue of artificial intelligence more prominently into the public awareness—where it is likely to remain.

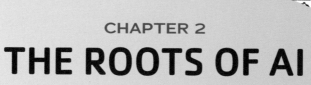

This nineteenth-century woodcut shows Charles Babbage's difference engine, a calculating machine designed in the 1820s. The machine was an early type of computer.

CHAPTER 2

THE ROOTS OF AI

Charles Babbage, often called the father of computing, was tired of doing calculations. In 1821 the British mathematician was double-checking numbers on charts used to predict the positions of stars and planets. To his great annoyance, the manually tabulated figures contained errors. "I wish to God these calculations had been executed by steam," grumbled Babbage, meaning that he wished the calculations had been made by a machine, such as a steam engine. (At the time, steam engines were revolutionizing manufacturing and transportation in Britain.)

According to historical lore, Babbage's frustration prompted him to design the primitive computer he called a difference engine. The blueprints called for cards punched with holes to be fed into a giant machine. The positioning of the holes would give the machine the data it needed to perform mathematical calculations.

Babbage's difference engine was never completed. If it had been, it would have had twenty-five thousand parts and weighed 4 tons (3.6 metric tons). It would have been enormous compared to modern computers, but in its design, it shared important features

A government staffer uses Herman Hollerith's tabulator to analyze census data in 1908. The machine greatly sped up compilation of the US census.

with them. Like modern computers, the difference engine contained a mechanism for inputting data, a memory system to store the data, a processor to perform calculations, and a way to output the results of the calculations.

Later in the nineteenth century, Herman Hollerith, a US statistician (someone who analyzes numeric data), assembled a

COMPUTER PIONEER: ADA LOVELACE

Unlike most nineteenth-century women, Ada Lovelace *(right)* received an excellent education. The daughter of a wealthy British family (her father was the poet Lord Byron and her mother was a baroness), she studied with a private tutor, focusing on science and mathematics. She also learned to read and speak French.

On June 5, 1833, when she was seventeen years old, she met Charles Babbage and saw a small-scale model of his difference engine. Nine years later, Lovelace read a French book about a more advanced machine that Babbage had designed, the analytical engine. Lovelace translated the work from French into English, adding detailed notes that went far beyond the original text. These notes, which were published in a British scientific journal, included an algorithm that is often considered the first published computer program.

Lovelace thought that the analytical engine could do more than mathematical calculations. She believed that it could also use mathematics to express music and language. But Lovelace drew the line at artificial intelligence. She did not believe that machines would ever be able to think on their own.

In the late 1970s, the US Department of Defense recognized Lovelace for her early contributions to computer science. It named a software language Ada in her honor. In the twenty-first century, the Association for Women in Computing honors women who excel in science and technology with the Ada Lovelace Awards.

calculating machine called a tabulator. Powered by electricity, the machine also used punch cards to analyze information. Like Babbage, Hollerith had a practical motivation for his invention. He worked for the US Census Bureau, which gathers statistics about Americans (such as their ages, marital status, ethnicity, and employment), and he wanted to summarize census results in less time. The 1880 census had taken clerks seven years to tally.

But using Hollerith's machines, clerks completed the 1890 census tally in just two years. By cutting down on labor costs, the machines saved the US government $5 million.

COMPUTERS AT WAR

In 1938 German mathematician Konrad Zuse built what many view as the first programmable computer, the Z1. Once again, punched holes fed information into the machine, but instead of cards, Zuse made holes in rolls of 35-millimeter film. The position of the holes told the computer what to do with the data it was receiving. Calculations were based on the binary numeral system, developed by another German, Gottfried Wilhelm Leibniz, in 1679. In the binary system, all numbers are represented by strings of 1s and 0s. For example, the number 5 is written as 101; the number 10 is 1010. The binary system is a good fit for computers, because computer circuits can be switched on or off to let electric current pass through. Zuse aligned the 1s and 0s of the binary system with the On and Off switches of his circuits. If a switch was turned on, it stood for 1. If a switch was turned off, it stood for 0. This approach enabled Zuse to process large amounts of data using just two digits.

Zuse was drafted into the German army during World War II (1939–1945), but he convinced army leaders to let him continue building computers rather than serve as a combat soldier. Funded by the German government's Aerodynamic Research Institute, he completed bigger and better versions of his computer, called the Z2 and the Z3. In 1940 Zuse proposed a high-speed computer that could be used to decipher secret messages from enemy countries intercepted by the Germans. But the machine would take more than a year to build, and German officials expected the war to be over by then. So they passed on Zuse's proposal.

During the war, the United Kingdom and Germany were on opposing sides. Unlike the German government, British officials were highly interested in using computers to crack enemy code. Three days after Germany invaded Poland on September 1, 1939, the beginning of the war,

BOMBE

A technician monitors a Bombe machine, which the British government used to decipher secret German messages during World War II. With information unscrambled by Bombes, British commanders knew what the enemy was planning.

computer pioneer and mathematician Alan Turing arrived at Bletchley Park in London. This was the headquarters for the top secret effort to decode intercepted German communications.

The German military used a machine called the Enigma to create its codes. First, the person running the machine typed the information to be shared. By turning a few wheels, the operator mixed up the order of the words and letters, which were then transmitted by radio. The person on the receiving end fed the message into another Enigma. Using a codebook, the operator duplicated the wheel settings that had been used to create the message, thereby unscrambling the words.

By the spring of 1940, Turing had developed a computer nicknamed the Bombe. Combining electronics and machine technology, the Bombe was capable of unraveling the Enigma codes. Three years later, Turing's

Bombes were decoding eighty-four thousand German messages a month, or two a minute.

The German army used a different machine, called Tunny, to scramble missives from the highest level of the German government, including those from dictator Adolf Hitler and his top military commanders. Turing found a way to unravel these messages too.

The Bletchley Park team built on Turing's work to create even more advanced computers. For instance, British engineer Thomas Flowers designed Colossus, hailed as the first electronic, programmable computer. Information supplied by Colossus helped the Allies—the United Kingdom and its partner nations (including the United States)—schedule D-day. This invasion of German-occupied France, on June 6, 1944, turned the tide of the war, leading the Allies to victory in 1945.

"WONDER BRAINS"

In the United States, too, World War II accelerated progress in computers. The US Army aimed its cannons and other big guns according to complicated charts called firing tables. But such tables could take weeks to create. To speed up the process, John Mauchly and J. Presper Eckert of the University of Pennsylvania built the Electronic Numerical Integrator and Computer (ENIAC). Although ENIAC was not completed until November 1945, after the war was over, the army used it for calculations for the next nine years.

Weighing 30 tons (27 metric tons) and 9 feet (2.7 m) high, the computer had eighteen thousand vacuum tubes and forty cabinets. It spread over an area the size of a small house. When the army went public with ENIAC on February 15, 1946, newspapers in the United States and Europe hailed it as an "electronic brain," a "wonder brain," and a "wizard," claims that were greatly exaggerated. ENIAC couldn't store programs in its memory, and it couldn't run more than one program at a time. Despite its drawbacks, ENIAC was an impressive machine that could add five thousand numbers per second. Computer historians estimate that between 1945 and

1955, ENIAC performed more calculations than had been done in the history of the world up to that time.

World War II had shown scientists the vast potential of computers. In the late 1940s, many scientists wanted to make the machines faster and more powerful. One of these researchers was John von Neumann, a Hungarian-born mathematician at the Institute for Advanced Study, an affiliate of Princeton University in Princeton, New Jersey. Von Neumann made a major contribution to the computer that succeeded ENIAC. Working with Mauchly and Eckert, he figured out how to store programs within computers. His plan became known as von Neumann architecture, and it formed the basis for future computer design. The basic structure consisted of a unit for processing data, a unit for storing data, and input and output devices.

Created to perform calculations for the US Army at the end of World War II, the Electronic Numerical Integrator and Computer (ENIAC) was a sprawling network of cabinets, cables, switches, vacuum tubes, and other equipment. Its programming and operation required a team of technicians.

As computers improved, researchers began to speculate about their potential. Some scientists said that given enough data, sophisticated hardware, and the right programming, computers might be able to learn, draw logical conclusions, and tackle intellectual challenges. A short anecdote about von Neumann illustrates the optimism of the era. After giving a talk on computers at Princeton University in 1948, von Neumann found himself facing a skeptical audience member. "Mere machines" would never be able to think, the man contended. Unfazed, von Neumann replied, "You insist that there is something a machine cannot do. If you will tell me *precisely* what it is that a machine cannot do, then I can always make a machine that will do just that!"

THINKING MACHINES

In January 1956, Herbert Simon, a professor at Carnegie Mellon University in Pittsburgh, made a remarkable announcement. "Over Christmas [my colleague] Allen Newell and I invented a thinking machine," he told his startled students. Although the device they called a Logic Theory Machine was not really self-aware in the way of humans, it solved geometry problems in ways that its inventors could not predict. With their third collaborator, J. C. Shaw, Simon and Newell would give the machine a theorem—a mathematical concept to be proved—and it would find the proof. The machine reached its own logical conclusions without step-by-step programming telling it what to do.

Only months after developing their machine, Simon and Newell carried the blueprint of their invention to Dartmouth College in New Hampshire. There, a small group of scientists led by Dartmouth professor John McCarthy had organized a summer workshop to study what they called artificial intelligence. However, this name for the emerging field of logical, reasoning machines struck some, including Simon and Newell, as not quite right. "The word *artificial* makes you think there's something kind of phony about this," another conference participant said years later, "or else it sounds like it's all artificial and there's nothing real about this work at all."

AI PIONEER: JOHN MCCARTHY

In the 1940s, when he was a student at the California Institute of Technology, John McCarthy attended a lecture by Hungarian American mathematician John von Neumann about "self-replicating automata," or machines that could make copies of themselves. (No such machines existed. Von Neumann's idea was just a theory.) After the lecture, McCarthy reasoned that a machine that could reproduce itself might be able to attain some form of intelligence. The idea stuck in his mind.

In 1964 McCarthy joined the faculty of Stanford University in California and founded the school's AI lab. At that time, he was optimistic that scientists could create an AI system within ten years. In later life, McCarthy had a more realistic view. Writing for the *Journal of the Association for Computing Machinery* in 2003, he set the odds of achieving artificial intelligence at "0.5 probability in the next 49 years, but a 0.25 probability that 49 years from now, the problems will be just as confusing as they are today."

The scientists spent some time debating what the new discipline should be called. "Complex information processing," "machine intelligence," and "automata studies" were all proposed yet failed to gain traction. In the end, the original term, *artificial intelligence*, proved to be the most memorable phrase after all.

The determined scientists crafted a very ambitious mission statement. They embraced the assumption that "every aspect of learning or any other feature of intelligence can in principle be so precisely described that a machine can be made to simulate [imitate] it." They aimed "to find how to make machines that use language, form . . . concepts, solve [the] kinds of problems now reserved for humans, and improve themselves." Then if a human could do it, so could a machine. The scientists expected to make a "significant advance" in at least one of their goals for machine awareness during that summer.

The members of the Dartmouth project greatly underestimated the challenges they faced. At the end of the summer, they were nowhere near the kind of self-improving machine they envisioned. But a new era in AI research was beginning. In 1959 McCarthy and Marvin Minsky, another scientist from the conference, founded the Artificial Intelligence Lab at the Massachusetts Institute of Technology (MIT) in Cambridge, Massachusetts. The two men soon became absorbed in finding ways to use LISP, a computer language that McCarthy had invented, in the pursuit of AI.

OFF TO A "SHAKEY" START

Meanwhile, in 1957, as AI scientists were working in relative obscurity, the Soviet Union (a nation that existed from 1922 to 1991 and included modern-day Russia) made headlines. The Soviets successfully launched Sputnik, the world's first artificial satellite that year.

The United States and the Soviet Union were then engaged in the bitter Cold War (1945–1991, a period of political, cultural, military, and economic rivalry and hostility). Stunned at the success of Sputnik, the US government sought ways to close the gap between US and Soviet technology. In 1958 President Dwight Eisenhower established the Advanced Research Projects Agency (ARPA), part of the US Department of Defense, to promote scientific research and to overtake the Soviet lead. The new organization funded promising scientific experiments and programs at US universities. This work included research into computers that would further US national defense and the space program.

Could artificial intelligence strengthen US security? Officials and generals at the Pentagon, US military headquarters near Washington, DC, thought that was possible. Believing that robots might be effective weapons, the government funded a project to build a robot that incorporated some of the latest advances in artificial intelligence. From 1966 to 1972, Charles Rosen of the Stanford Research Institute at Stanford University led the project. Rosen's team produced a 5-foot-tall (1.5 m), battery-powered rolling robot topped with a television camera, microphone, and radio antenna. Behind the scenes, the robot also consisted of a computer that filled an entire room. A second, smaller computer acted as an interface between the large mechanical "brain" in the backroom and the robot. Fortified with "intelligence" provided by the computer, the robot could plan its own route through the laboratory. A television camera and a sonar range finder (a device that uses sound waves to determine an object's location) enabled the robot to sense objects in its path. When it did, the robot stood still for several minutes before "deciding" how to move around the obstruction. The robot had a degree of independence, but it was far from perfect. Its batteries ran down quickly, and it needed frequent repairs. And it quivered as it moved, which led researchers to name it Shakey.

Despite Shakey's flaws, the public eagerly embraced it as a revolutionary marvel. An enthusiastic article in the November 1970 issue of *Life* magazine made the robot famous as the world's "first electronic person." Grossly exaggerating Shakey's capabilities, the writer said that the robot

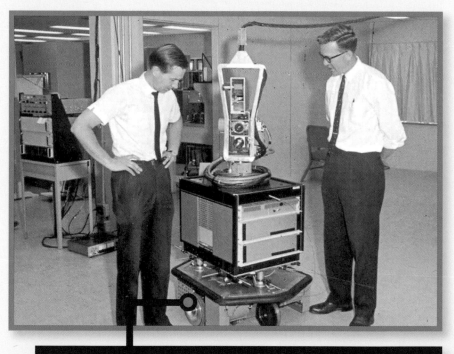

Created in the era before microprocessors and personal computers, Shakey was a clunky robot that disappointed its US government funders. Here Sven Wahlstrom *(left)* and Nils Nilsson *(right)*, members of the team that built Shakey at Stanford University, inspect the robot.

SHAKEY'S LEGACY

Despite the cancellation of the Shakey project, the robot left an important legacy to AI research. For instance, methods developed to enable Shakey to navigate around obstacles contributed later to mapping technology, such as the Global Positioning System (GPS) software for modern smartphones and cars.

After the Shakey project shut down, the robot was stored at Stanford University. But in 1987, the Computer Museum in Boston put Shakey on display in its Smart Machines Theater (later called the Robot Theater). When the Boston museum closed in 2000, Shakey returned to California, along with some other robots. Since 2011 it has been displayed at the Computer History Museum in Mountain View, California.

zipped down hallways faster than most humans walked and that it was able to reason about its environment. Such excessive claims upset many AI scientists, who did not like to see their work overhyped.

The Pentagon was not as impressed with the results of the Shakey project. "Can you mount a 36-inch [91-centimeter] bayonet on [Shakey]?" one general asked. A robot with a gun could be helpful to the military. A robot that could navigate hallways had little practical use in the eyes of top generals. Dissatisfied with the pace of progress, government officials stopped funding the Shakey project in 1972.

Although researchers had made progress in weak AI, systems that performed limited tasks, a strong intelligence that could think and act independently remained far in the future. To make AI succeed, researchers needed better computer hardware, faster processors, and more data than was then available. Losing faith in artificial intelligence, officials in Washington, DC, stopped allocating funds for additional AI projects. A period known as the AI Winter—a time of limited funding and reduced activity—had set in. For many years, the pendulum would swing back and forth between AI Winters and bursts of renewed activity and optimism.

In founding Microsoft, Bill Gates *(left)* and Paul Allen *(right)* set the stage for the personal computer revolution. The surge in computer technology in the late twentieth century gave a boost to AI technology as well.

THE PC REVOLUTION

While AI research stagnated, the business sector made great strides in computer technology. Computers became smaller and easier to use. Corporations embraced new computers that allowed them to keep detailed accounts of product inventories and business transactions. In 1971 Ted Hoff, an engineer at Intel, a technology company in Santa Clara, California, invented the microprocessor. A processor organizes information and directs the workings of a computer, and a microprocessor is just what the name implies—a tiny processor. Hoff's microprocessor was mounted on a silicon chip no bigger than a fingernail, but it had as much computing power as the enormous ENIAC had twenty-five years earlier.

Thanks to microprocessors, computers became increasingly smaller and less expensive. In 1975 Harvard University students Bill Gates and Paul G. Allen founded a software company that would soon become a household name—Microsoft. Steve Jobs and Stephen Wozniak met while working on a large business computer at the information technology company Hewlett-Packard in the early 1970s. They created a small computer called Apple I in 1976. A few years later, Microsoft created an operating system for personal computers (PCs) built by IBM and other technology companies.

The new personal computers were small enough to fit on a desktop. They allowed students, business owners, and other individuals to create and edit documents, manage financial data, perform complicated calculations, and do myriad other tasks. Soon millions of consumers in the United States and other wealthy nations were buying personal computers. The industry grew so fast that *Time* magazine named the PC its Man of the Year in 1982.

THE NEXT GENERATION

The PC revolution led to many innovations and ambitious undertakings. In 1982 the Japanese Ministry of International Trade and Industry launched its Fifth Generation computer project. The goal was to develop superfast computers with the ability to reason and the potential to understand language, diagnose diseases, and analyze legal documents.

The prospect of Japan outpacing the United States in computer technology alarmed many government officials. "It may be unfortunate, but we are in a science race," said David Brandin of the US Commerce

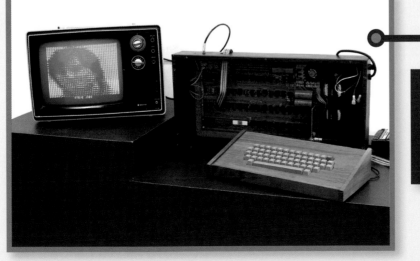

In 1976 Steve Jobs and Stephen Wozniak built a few hundred computers like this one and sold them to other computer hobbyists. They called the machines Apples.

Department in 1984. "The question is, who will be the first commercial exploiter of [the next generation of] computer technologies." To remain competitive, US officials decided once again to support the development of artificial intelligence. The United Kingdom and several other European countries also funded AI projects.

A great deal of hope and optimism surrounded the Fifth Generation and other AI efforts in the 1980s and early 1990s. But after ten years and a $400 million investment, the Japanese Fifth Generation program and similar programs in other countries failed to produce intelligent computers.

Despite these disappointments, computer scientists were making progress in another form of artificial intelligence, expert systems. Pioneered by Edward Feigenbaum of Stanford University, these systems store vast amounts of information about a specific field, such as business or medicine. Engineers feed this data, as well as step-by-step instructions, into a computer. Computers then can draw conclusions from the data. The computer's task might involve evaluating the stock market or analyzing a chemical compound. Expert systems represent the "top-down" approach to AI. By giving a computer data and sets of rules for drawing conclusions from that data, researchers are essentially telling it what to do.

FORWARD MOMENTUM

British computer scientist Timothy Berners-Lee, inventor of the World Wide Web (which he completed in 1990), recalls a favorite saying of his computer pioneer parents. When he was growing up, they asserted that "what you could do with the computer was limited only by your imagination."

During the 1990s, computer scientists seemed to justify that view by pushing the boundaries of computer capability. They created tremendous improvements in word processing and language translation programs. They developed sophisticated graphics and gaming programs. In 1990 Massachusetts-based Dragon Systems made headlines when it introduced a program that converted spoken words into text on a computer screen. With this program, users with disabilities that prevented them from typing or using a mouse could use vocal commands to control a computer.

As the decade wore on, the World Wide Web and the Internet began to transform the modern world. (The Internet is a network of networks, connecting millions of computers together. The World Wide Web consists of systems that allow people to access, post to, and interact with websites on the Internet.) Meanwhile, technology companies were building faster and faster computers with more and more memory. These two developments—increases in computer power and the enormous amounts of data uploaded to the Internet by countless individuals worldwide—would have a major impact on the development of artificial intelligence.

As the decade wore on, the World Wide Web and the Internet began to transform the modern world.

CHAPTER 3

DEEP LEARNING

Scientists at Google X, a semisecret division of the famous technology company, are known for thinking big. High-altitude Wi-Fi balloons, contact lenses that monitor blood-sugar levels, and self-driving cars are just some of the ambitious projects the Google X team has tackled.

In 2011 the researchers embarked on perhaps the greatest challenge of all: Google Brain, an electronic simulation of a human brain. The Google Brain team used sixteen thousand computer processors to create a latticelike structure of more than one billion connections. Led by computer scientist Andrew Ng, and Google researcher Jeff Dean, the team attempted to mimic (on a much smaller scale) neural networks, or the complex interrelationship of nerve cells in the human brain.

Without telling their electronic brain how to recognize images, researchers showered it with ten million randomly chosen thumbnails from YouTube videos for three days. Then they presented the brain with a list of twenty thousand categories for sorting out the objects shown in the thumbnails. What happened next made headlines. Google's artificial brain began to identify cats. No one had programmed the brain to look for tails, whiskers, or pointed ears in the thumbnails. All on its own, it had developed the concept of "cat," and it recognized cats in the pictures with almost 75 percent accuracy. Its success rate in correctly labeling images as human faces was even higher.

With no previous knowledge of what cats look like, an artificial neural network called Google Brain taught itself to recognize pictures of cats. Andrew Ng led the Google Brain team.

The researchers were stunned. They had created an artificial intelligence that was able to develop its own working knowledge of the world. Unlike top-down machines, which process only the data given to them, using only instructions provided by programmers, Google Brain had figured out what to do and drawn its own conclusions. This is an example of a bottom-up artificial intelligence.

In this 1950s neural network, electronic signals traveled through wires in imitation of the way electronic signals travel through neurons in the human brain.

NEURAL NETWORKS

Although the success of Google Brain and other artificial neural networks is a relatively recent phenomenon, the idea of simulating a human brain goes back to 1951. In that year, roboticist Marvin Minsky and his Princeton University colleague Dean Edmonds set out to design an electronic system that would replicate some of the human brain's thought processes.

The functioning of the human brain was (and continues to be) a mystery in many ways, but researchers had some basic facts. They knew that a human brain has about one hundred billion neurons, or nerve cells. Each neuron has thousands of connections to other neurons. Electrical signals enter neurons through elongated branches called dendrites, and electrical signals exit each neuron through a single fiber called an axon. In this way, signals travel from one neuron to another.

Minsky and Edmonds built a machine with only forty artificial neurons—a far cry from the human brain's one hundred billion. Called SNARC (which stands for Stochastic Neural Analog Reinforcement Calculator), the machine is generally considered the first artificial neural network.

A FITTING OBIT

When Marvin Minsky died in 2016, long obituaries, detailing his many contributions to the field of AI, appeared in newspapers. But a very brief obituary that appeared in *Wired* magazine might have pleased him more than the lengthier eulogies. The following is an excerpt:

> Marvin Minsky was known for his pioneer contribution to the field of artificial intelligence (AI). After graduating from Phillips Academy, Minsky attended Harvard University, graduating with a BA in Mathematics in 1950. He continued his education at Princeton University, ultimately graduating with a PhD in Mathematics in 1954. Some of Minsky's greatest accomplishments include founding the MIT Computer Science and Artificial Intelligence Laboratory in 1959 and authoring many groundbreaking books in the field of artificial intelligence, including *Perceptrons*. He won many notable awards in his field of study, including the Turing Award in 1969.

Who wrote the obituary? The writer wasn't a "who" at all. Wordsmith, a newswriting bot (short for *robot*) developed by the company Automated Insights, wrote the tribute to Minsky. Humans fed biographical data into the bot, and it created the text.

In this photo from the early 1980s, Marvin Minsky demonstrates an interactive glove used to control a robot's movements.

Five years later, in 1956, Frank Rosenblatt at Cornell University in Ithaca, New York, led another effort to mimic the human brain. He and his team devised a system called the Perceptron, which received visual information and attempted to identify it. The system involved three levels of artificial nerve cells that worked together to classify images. The first level consisted of photoelectric cells (electronic devices that respond to changes in light) that captured images. The second level contained connector cells that received input from the photocells. The third level contained output cells that labeled the images.

The three layers interacted simply. A photocell would capture an image, such as a picture of a dog. Connector cells would route the image to random cells in the third layer. These output cells would label the image, choosing from a list of categories provided by the research team. If the Perceptron correctly identified the image as a dog, scientists would strengthen the electrical connections between the cells that had led to that answer. This made it more likely for the "dog" connection to be activated the next time the system encountered a picture of a dog. The stronger such connections became, the more the system "learned."

Rosenblatt's work generated a great deal of buzz. In July 1958, the *New York Times* hailed the Perceptron, rather too optimistically, as "a machine which senses, recognizes, remembers and responds like the human mind." Rosenblatt also made some dramatic claims about its capabilities. But not all AI researchers agreed with such glowing assessments. "To hear [Rosenblatt] tell it," one scientist reported, "the Perceptron was capable of fantastic things. And maybe it was. But you couldn't prove it by the work [he] did."

Disappointed in his own work as well as Rosenblatt's, Marvin Minsky was among those who took the cautious view. In 1969 Minsky and his colleague Seymour Papert published the book *Perceptrons*, which criticized artificial neural networks and denied that they could ever live up to the claims made for them. Interest in neural networks faded rapidly as researchers turned to other AI models, such as the top-down approach.

"THE MACHINE CODE OF THE BRAIN"

The idea of a biology-inspired approach to artificial intelligence did not disappear completely. Geoffrey Hinton, a British graduate student at the University of Edinburgh in Scotland, was fascinated by the human mind and wanted to create a learning machine based on the human brain. In the mid-1970s, however, he could not find professors receptive to his ideas. "Don't you get it?" his teachers told him. "[Neural networks] are no good."

But Hinton refused to be dissuaded. In 1982 Hinton organized a summer conference about AI. Although he expected that most participants would favor the more formal, top-down approach to machine learning, he also hoped to attract fresh ideas. He printed a brochure, offering to cover the conference costs for anyone with novel suggestions. One application caught his attention at once. A young researcher named Terry Sejnowski professed to know the "machine code of the brain." Hinton wondered if the applicant was delusional or brilliant.

When the two men met at the conference, they found they shared a similar vision of neural networks. Although Hinton by then worked at Carnegie Mellon University in Pittsburgh and Sejnowski was at Johns Hopkins University in Baltimore, Maryland, they became friends and managed to get together on weekends. In 1985 they developed a new kind of neural network with more layers than previous ones had used. Called a Boltzmann machine, the network used a mathematical approach invented by Austrian physicist Ludwig Boltzmann and it "learned" in a way similar to humans—by drawing conclusions from the data it was exposed to.

Would this new approach to AI work better than established top-down models? Sejnowski decided to prove its worth by teaching the Boltzmann machine to pronounce English words and sentences. He programmed the network with rules on pronunciation taken from a large textbook. But as Hinton pointed out to him, "English is an incredibly complicated language and your simple network won't be able to absorb it." So the two men hit upon a plan. Just as a child proceeds from easier to more complex tasks, their machine would first try to pronounce words from a simple children's book.

Sejnowski and Hinton fed the book's limited vocabulary into the machine, and about an hour later, it began to emit sounds through the speaker to which it was attached. At first, the syllables sounded like a baby learning to talk. But soon Sejnowski and Hinton began to make out words. The network kept working and learning until it was able to pronounce every word in the book perfectly. Soon it graduated to a story told by a fifth grader and finally to a twenty-thousand-word dictionary. Running through a powerful computer, the network taught itself how to pronounce more and more words. Sejnowski and Hinton named its language NetTalk.

DEEP LEARNING

Although the Boltzmann machine showed remarkable results, the larger AI community continued to focus on the rule-based, top-down approach. Using this approach in the late twentieth century, AI researchers created systems that could understand speech, analyze images, and produce clear, grammatical sentences. Neural networks were mostly considered a dead end, even as a very small number of dedicated researchers made progress.

The tide turned in 2006 when Hinton's neural networks began to outperform more established, top-down systems in processing speech and images. Hinton and a PhD student named Ruslan Salakhutdinov published their findings about the new networks, which had many more layers and connections than earlier machines. Because of these extra layers, the systems were said to be deep, and their achievements were dubbed deep learning. Google Brain is an example of deep learning.

In deep learning, a researcher feeds a large amount of data into a neural network running on a computer. This data might consist of millions of handwritten alphabet letters or numbers. The network is tasked with "guessing" which numbers look most alike and sorting them accordingly. Correct guesses result in reinforced neural connections. Progressing from simpler to more complex classifications, the neural network goes from recognizing letters to deciphering words. Since no teacher tells it exactly what to do, this approach is called unsupervised learning.

Deep learning is a far cry from human learning. Ben Medlock, cofounder and chief technology officer of the British AI startup company SwiftKey, points out that neural networks require an enormous amount of data to become skilled at a task or to recognize images. But humans require very few examples. For instance, Google Brain processed millions of images to learn to identify cats. A small child has to see only a few cats to learn to recognize them.

Neural networks have made some surprising mistakes. They have labeled images of music concerts as spiders and labeled pictures of ducks as US president Barack Obama. In 2012 neural networks could correctly identify less than one-sixth of the pictures in the data they were fed. Despite such limitations, the networks are able to outperform earlier AI systems in many ways, and they continue to get better. The huge amount of information available through the Internet contributes greatly to these improvements. The Internet allows researchers to train neural networks using virtually unlimited amounts of data.

The Internet allows researchers to train neural networks using virtually unlimited amounts of data.

SILICON VALLEY TAKES NOTE

In November 2012, an audience in Tianjin, China, got a chance to experience the power of deep learning firsthand. Richard Rashid, head scientist at Microsoft, was giving a talk on speech recognition and neural networks in a huge auditorium. As he spoke, his words appeared in English on a large screen. After each sentence, Rashid paused slightly to give a neural network the few seconds it needed to translate his written English words into Chinese characters and then to imitate his voice in Mandarin Chinese. The spectators had never seen anything like it. Their enthusiastic applause was as much for deep learning as it was for Rashid's actual speech.

ALPHAGO

When a computer beats a human in games, it's big news. Deep Blue's victory over human chess champion Garry Kasparov in 1997 made worldwide headlines. Watson's win on *Jeopardy!* garnered IBM lots of publicity. In an even more significant milestone, in March 2016, Google's deep learning software AlphaGo beat South Korean grandmaster Lee Sedol four out of five games in the ancient Chinese game of go.

Although it's fairly easy to learn to play go, the number of possible playing piece positions surpasses the number of atoms in the universe. That number is between 10^{78} (1 with 78 zeros behind it) and 10^{82} (1 with 82 zeros behind it). Sheer computing power is insufficient to deal with such figures. Instead, human go players rely on reasoning and intuition in choosing their moves.

To beat Sedol, AlphaGo also used reasoning and intuition. Geoffrey Hinton explains, "With these neural networks, computers can do that too. They can think about all the possible moves and think that one particular move seems a bit better than the others, just intuitively."

Lee Sedol, a grandmaster player, took on Google's AlphaGo computer program at a go tournament in March 2016. Sedol lost to the computer four games out of five.

News of the spectacular demonstration greatly boosted interest in deep learning. Businesses in Silicon Valley—a region south of San Francisco, California, that is home to hundreds of technology companies, including Google, Apple, and Facebook—took note. Everyone was talking about the exciting new AI technology.

Start-up tech companies began incorporating deep learning into the services they offered. So did major tech businesses such as Facebook, IBM, Yahoo, Microsoft, and the Chinese company Baidu. Geoffrey Hinton himself accepted a job at Google. That company's 2014 acquisition of the London-based AI company DeepMind for $400 million sent ripples through the industry and accelerated the already keen competition to develop the most powerful AI. Investors poured millions of dollars into deep learning companies.

Once rejected as impractical, neural networks have become the cutting edge of AI research. Not only can these networks learn to recognize objects and understand speech, they can also help robots identify items in their paths and maneuver around them. Researchers believe that neural networks will soon be used to predict stock market trends, compose music, analyze genetic data, and diagnose medical problems.

How far artificial intelligence can advance with deep learning remains to be seen, but researchers are optimistic. "The point about [deep learning] is that it scales [gets more effective the larger it gets] beautifully," Geoffrey Hinton told John Markoff of the *New York Times* in 2012. "Basically you just need to keep making it bigger and faster, and it will get better. There's no looking back now." Two years later, Hinton enthused in *Wired* magazine, "We want to take AI . . . to wonderful new places." Modifying the slogan from *Star Trek*, he added that he hoped to see AI technology go "where no person, no student, no program has gone before."

CHAPTER 4

THE RISE OF ROBOTS

The idea of humanlike machines has intrigued humans for centuries. As early as 1495, Italian painter Leonardo da Vinci, famous for his scientific vision as well as his artistic masterpieces, designed a contraption called a mechanical knight. Through an elaborate system of pulleys, cables, and gears, da Vinci's knight was able to sit down, stand up, walk, and even wave. It was as if a metal man had come to life.

More than four hundred years later, another metal man delighted visitors at the 1939–1940 World's Fair in New York City. Elektro, a 7-foot

(2.1 m), 265-pound (120 kg) "moto man" could walk, shake his head, and move his hands. He could blow up balloons and smoke cigarettes. Even more astonishing, he could talk with spectators, answering their questions and telling jokes. Sparko, his metal dog, also entertained viewers with his mechanical antics.

Elektro wasn't unique. Throughout the 1920s and 1930s, engineers had been experimenting with robots. Although these machines fascinated the public, they had no more self-awareness than any other piece of mechanical equipment. Elektro's words came from record players connected to his body. None of the spectators who interacted with him really believed that a machine could make its own conversation.

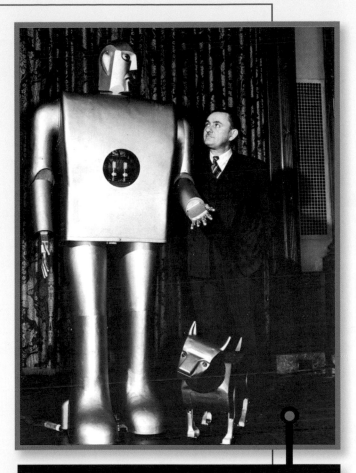

Elektro, a mechanical man, delighted visitors at the 1939–1940 World's Fair in New York City. So did his mechanical dog, Sparko. Elektro was nothing like modern-day robots, which perform repetitive tasks and which in some cases have artificial intelligence. At the time of the fair, such robots were many decades in the future.

ROBOTS IN POP CULTURE

From Rosie, the clunky-looking mechanical maid of the 1960s cartoon series *The Jetsons*, to the shockingly realistic humanoids of the 2015 AMC series *Humans*, robots have delighted and frightened audiences for decades. On the positive side, Robby the Robot, star of the 1956 movie *Forbidden Planet*, proved so popular that the robot with a bubble-shaped head made cameo appearances in television shows. A decade after Robby's debut, the more technically named B-9 Environmental Control Robot of the TV series *Lost in Space* gained fame for its humor and anxious protection of the Robinson family as it repeatedly cautioned, "Danger, Will Robinson, Danger!" Fans of *Star Trek: The Next Generation*, which aired in the 1980s, will never forget the complexity and the charm of the android Data. Logical but longing to "one day . . . discover [his] own humanity," Data was able to tap dance, paint, and perform sixty trillion mathematical calculations per second. His intellect and capacity to tap directly into databanks of computers saved the starship *Enterprise* on several occasions.

On the dark side, the popular *Terminator* movies feature Skynet, a sentient supercomputer that wages war on its creators by unleashing machines programmed with a single objective: "Kill All Humans." That's also the goal of the evil AI agent Archos in Daniel H. Wilson's best-selling novel *Robopocalypse*. The list of good and bad robots in popular culture goes on and on. For good or for evil, the only limit on science fiction robots is the imagination of authors and filmmakers.

The 1960s cartoon TV series *The Jetsons* featured a family of the future with a robotic maid named Rosie.

But the idea of robots with artificial intelligence still captivated the human imagination. Throughout the twentieth century, robots were a staple in science fiction. The word *robot* entered the English language in 1923 with the translation of Czech author Karel Capek's play *R.U.R*, or *Rossum's Universal Robots*. In this play, the mechanical creatures did not resemble Elektro. Instead of metal, they were made of a substance that mimicked living tissue, so they looked exactly like biological humans. Their creators made them work in factories, fight wars, clean homes—whatever needed doing. However, what started out as a beneficial scenario for humanity turned desperate when the robots decided to rise up against their masters. The play, ending on a bleak note, started a literary tradition of robots attempting to take over Earth.

A very different concept of robots emerged a few decades later when acclaimed science fiction writer Isaac Asimov published his short story "Runaround." Asimov envisioned a species of well-behaved artificial beings bound by three laws of robotics:

1. A robot may not injure a human being or, through inaction, allow a human being to come to harm.
2. A robot must obey the orders given it by human beings except where such orders would conflict with the First Law.
3. A robot must protect its own existence as long as such protection does not conflict with the First or Second Law.

Asimov's robots were admirable and trustworthy. So too were many later film and TV robots, including B-9 from the 1960s TV show *Lost in Space* and R2-D2 and C-3PO of the *Star Wars* movies. But other fictional robots, such as the robot masters of *The Matrix* films, were sinister.

ONE SIMPLE DIRECTION AFTER ANOTHER

While science fiction fans enjoyed reading about robots in books and seeing them on the screen, engineers were designing real robots that did actual work. The first robots were cumbersome, however. Like Shakey, they took in information through sensors and fed it to an external computer. The computer figured out what the robot should do and sent it instructions. The process was slow and inefficient, and robots were easily overwhelmed with too much information.

Working at the Artificial Intelligence Lab at MIT in the 1980s, Australian scientist Rodney Brooks realized that robots would be more effective if they could process data on their own, without external computers. He also believed that robots should be given one simple direction after another instead of being bombarded with information.

Inspired by the simplicity of mosquitoes, Brooks began patterning tiny robots after insects. In 1988 he created a groundbreaking robot named Genghis. The six-legged robot, measuring about 13.8 inches (35 cm) long and weighing just 2.2 pounds (1 kg), could climb and walk, moving faster than most other robots. With sensors to detect heat coming from the human body, it could also follow people around. The tiny machine changed the way robots were built and paved the way for useful robots in hospitals and factories.

ROBOTS AT WORK

In 1990 Brooks founded the company iRobot and went on to invent the popular robotic vacuum cleaner Roomba. The flat round disk is able to sense and skirt objects in its path as it sucks up dirt. Brooks launched a new company, Rethink Robotics, in 2008. Four years later, the company introduced Baxter, a robot created to perform strenuous tasks, such as loading boxes. The 165-pound (75 kg), 37-inch-tall (0.9 m) robot has two arms and a computer screen (complete with digital "eyes") for a face. Three years after Baxter, its "younger brother" Sawyer made its debut. Much lighter than Baxter and with only one arm, Sawyer is designed for precision tasks, such as testing circuit boards and tending machines. Like other robots, Sawyer and Baxter don't tire out and can work around the clock. They don't get bored by performing the same task over and over.

These qualities make them especially suited for the repetitive nature of factory work.

The Tesla auto manufacturing plant in Fremont, California, provides an exceptionally good example of what working robots can accomplish. At Tesla more than one hundred robots of different shapes and sizes work with humans to assemble electric cars. Named after characters from *X-Men* comic books, the robots perform a variety of specialized tasks. Towering over their biological coworkers, Wolverine and Iceman hoist entire vehicles from one assembly line to another. Other robots put seats into cars and install windshields. Some robots do their work while dangling from the ceiling. Others transport materials throughout the plant.

Robots are also at work at Amazon.com fulfillment centers, or warehouses. When you order a product from the online retailer, there's a

At a Tesla auto plant in Fremont, California, robots do much of the work of assembling electric cars. Some fear that robots will take over more and more workplace tasks, leaving fewer jobs for humans. Others point out that businesses will always need human workers to design, program, and repair robots. In addition, robot intelligence can't match human intelligence or replace human decision making.

good chance a robot will pick it off the warehouse shelf. In 2012 Amazon bought the robotics company Kiva Systems, which had developed robots for picking and packing products at warehouses, for more than $750 million. Three years later, Amazon boasted thirty thousand Kiva robots in fifteen of its fulfillment centers. The squat metal machines receive orders to retrieve items from a vast area of tall, square shelving towers called pods. A robot on its way to pick an item must pass around and under these towers until it reaches the pod with the required item. Sliding under the tower, the robot lifts the stack of shelves onto its back. Lugging its tall load, it once again scoots across the floor, this time, to a human worker who removes the needed object. Then the robot transports the pod back to its original location. Tracking software coordinates the process.

"THE CUSP OF EXPLODING"

More and more industries and professions are turning to robots to cut labor costs and increase efficiency. "We have a firm belief that the robotics market is on the cusp of exploding," said Texas Instruments vice president Remi El-Ouazzane in 2012.

According to computer scientist Jerry Kaplan, author of *Humans Need Not Apply: A Guide to Wealth and Work in the Age of Artificial Intelligence*, several factors are responsible for the dramatic progress in robotics. First, the computers that run robots are more powerful than ever before, and deep learning techniques make them smarter. Improved designs allow robots to react more quickly when they encounter obstacles, while lighter-weight materials make them less cumbersome. Finally, developments in machine perception allow robots to scan images and to correctly identify faces, inanimate (nonliving) objects, and movements—advances that help robots interact meaningfully with humans.

Kaplan expects to see robots of the future weeding gardens, picking crops, painting houses, carrying packages, and even directing traffic. In the Netherlands and Belgium, robots named Hector are helping some senior citizens with daily activities. Described by one journalist as "a big, walking and talking smartphone," Hector was designed by a team at the University of Reading in the United Kingdom. The robot can pick up objects, make grocery lists, and remind its owner to take medicines, among other activities. At a hospital in San Francisco, robots called Tugs deliver meals, medicines, and clean bed linen to patients' rooms. Equipped with lasers and sensors to navigate around obstacles, Tugs use radio waves to open doors in hospital corridors and use the hospital's Wi-Fi network to call elevators.

SUPERHUMAN SURGERY

Hospital robots do much more than mundane tasks. The da Vinci Surgical System, made by the US company Intuitive Surgical (and named for Leonardo da Vinci), allows doctors to operate on patients with greater exactness than can be achieved by hand. Incisions made by the da Vinci machine tend to be smaller than those made by a human surgeon. Generally, smaller and more precise incisions translate into more rapid patient recovery after surgery. Around the world, doctors used da Vinci systems to perform 650,000 surgical procedures in 2015.

A da Vinci Surgical System costs $1.8 million and weighs more than 1,000

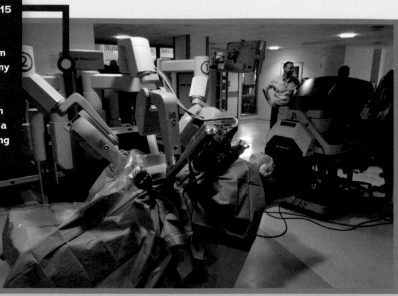

This display at a 2015 science fair in Great Britain shows a da Vinci Surgical System operating on a dummy patient. The robotic instruments can perform surgery with more precision than a human doctor working by hand.

pounds (454 kg). Surgeons operating in war zones need something lighter, more mobile, and less expensive. To meet this need, engineers Jacob Rosen of the University of California–Santa Cruz and Blake Hannaford of the University of Washington developed such a robot, called the Raven, in 2005. A newer version of the Raven, Raven II, is even smaller than its predecessor and operates with more precision. It can perform many kinds of operations, including heart surgery. Gregory Hager, a computer scientist at Johns Hopkins University, has called the Raven an "opportunity to go from what humans can do, to doing things that are really superhuman. And to do superhuman surgery will require robots to have enough intelligence to recognize what the surgeon is doing and to offer appropriate assistance. . . . All of that is coming down the road."

WHAT'S NEXT?

According to the research firm International Data Corporation, businesses around the world spent $71 billion on robotics in 2015. This money went to purchase robots and the software that runs them and even to pay for services such as robotic receptionists. The two industries with the fastest growth rate in robotics are health care and manufacturing. Spending on robotics is expected to skyrocket to $135.4 billion by 2019.

But robots come with a downside. The danger is not, as some science fiction writers imagine, that robots will take over Earth. The fear is that robots will take jobs from humans. The process has already begun, with factory positions and telecommunications work becoming automated, and it is likely to continue. In 2016 US government economists issued some sobering statistics. They predicted that workers earning less than $20 per hour—holding jobs that do not require much schooling and therefore come with low pay—have an 83 percent chance of being replaced by robots. Those who earn more money (because their jobs require more schooling and skill and are not as easily performed by machines) face a reduced risk. Some experts fear that displaced workers won't be able to find new jobs. The government report notes that a worst-case scenario would "lead to vast increases in income inequality, masses of people who are effectively unemployable, and breakdowns in the social order."

Others disagree. Richard Morris, a vice president with the car company BMW, believes humans will always play a vital role in the workforce. Businesses will always need workers to program, monitor, and service the robots. In the Tesla factory, about three thousand human workers greatly outnumber the robots. And despite great advances in robotics, researchers are nowhere near producing a machine that is animated by strong artificial intelligence. No robot can think for itself or set its own goals. Whether it's vacuuming a floor, exploring the ocean floor, performing surgery, or manufacturing cars, robots are narrowly tailored to perform specific tasks. "Ideas come from people," Morris states, "and a robot is never going to replace that." Real-life robots liberate workers from tedious or dangerous jobs, but so far, they cannot replicate human ingenuity.

Often called the father of modern robotics, Rodney Brooks agrees that much of the anxiety about robots taking over jobs is misplaced. "The robot can't do everything a person can do—just like an electric drill doesn't replace a contractor. Robots can only do certain things, and they're letting the person do the more cognitive parts [the thinking]. We're undervaluing [the abilities of human] workers when we say that robots are replacing them."

CHAPTER 5

ROBOTS IN EXTREME SITUATIONS

On September 11, 2001 (9/11), terrorists hijacked four commercial airplanes and flew two of them into the World Trade Center's twin towers in New York City and one into the Pentagon, US military headquarters near Washington, DC. A fourth jet crashed in a field in Pennsylvania after passengers fought back against the hijackers.

In New York, the twin towers burned and collapsed after the planes struck them. The collapsed buildings presented an overwhelming challenge to emergency workers and rescue crews. How could they search the dangerous mountains of rubble for survivors? The spaces that workers needed to investigate were largely airless and impossibly tight. At the site of each building, 110 stories had collapsed into the height of about 10 stories and fires had ignited in the debris. Yet deep within the ruins could lie air pockets still capable of supporting life. Watching the disaster unfold on television, Robin Murphy, then a professor of computer science at the University of South Florida, realized the magnitude of the dilemma. But she knew a way to help. She knew that robots could explore places inaccessible to human rescuers. Within hours, Murphy sprang into action.

Murphy's team was one of four robot teams that rushed to the disaster. Another team came from iRobot. According to iRobot's Joe Dyer, his company's PackBots were "literally pulled out of the laboratory and taken to [the World Trade Center site]." Operated by remote control, the 24-pound (10.9 kg), 7-inch-high (18 cm) PackBots sifted through the rubble, maneuvering into tight positions, testing the stability of mounds of debris, and sending back photos to human handlers. Special sensors allowed the robots to detect gases from hazardous materials. Guided by remote control, they created channels through the wreckage that made excavation easier for human rescuers. The PackBots did not find any survivors, but they made a dangerous job safer for rescue crews.

FEARLESS AND EFFICIENT

Since 9/11, rescuers have used robots in almost every major disaster throughout the world. When Hurricane Katrina devastated New Orleans in 2005, small flying robots equipped with cameras searched for survivors in buildings surrounded by floodwaters. Five years later, in 2010, an oil rig exploded in the Gulf of Mexico and millions of barrels of oil seeped into the Gulf from an undersea well. During the spill, scientists used underwater robots called Seagliders to assess the damaged well. The 6-foot-long (1.8 m) robots could dive to 3,300 feet (1,006 km), a depth at which human divers would be killed by the pressure of the water above them. Several times a day, the robots surfaced to send vital information to scientists monitoring the spill.

Thinking especially of Seagliders, Dyer once praised robots in action as "fearless . . . very cost-effective and efficient." Such qualities make robots attractive to use in situations that are dangerous, including military missions, space exploration, and environmental disasters. For example, a tsunami (a giant ocean wave) hit the Fukushima Daiichi Nuclear Power Plant in Japan in March 2011, seriously weakening the facility and releasing high levels of radiation inside the structure. Because radiation can be deadly, humans couldn't enter the damaged facility. So to assist the Japanese authorities, the US Defense Advanced Research Projects Agency (DARPA, the successor to ARPA) sent PackBots and other robots—equipped with radiation shielding to protect their electronic parts—to survey the damage and to monitor radiation levels.

But problems ensued. First, technicians at the plant needed instructions on how to use the robots. By the time their training was complete, radioactive materials had generated so much heat that steel structures supporting the building had melted. This damage allowed radiation to leak from the facility into the environment outside. When the robots finally entered the building, they surveyed the devastation on the ground floor and registered levels of radiation well above the safety limit for humans. But

ROBOTIC SENSORS

To act autonomously, or without human controllers telling them what to do, robots need sensory input from their environment. They need to "see" objects around them, which they can by using cameras, light sensors, and photosensitive cells. They need to "hear" what is happening, with information coming from microphones. Depending on its function, a robot may also need to sense heat, sense pressure, or pick up on other environmental cues. "Robots are gaining human capabilities," noted robotics graduate student Daniel H. Wilson in 2013, "whether it's smell or touch or recognizing our voices. If they are going to solve human problems, they will have to have human abilities."

A sense of "smell" will be crucial for robots in hazardous environments. For example, robots might help human workers pinpoint leakages of methane (an explosive gas) at landfills or locate other dangerous gases after earthquakes and accidents. Achim Lilienthal at Örebro University in Sweden has invented a machine called Gasbot that uses lasers to locate distant clouds of gas. Resembling a riding lawnmower with an eyeball on top, Gasbot determines the concentration of gases and creates a 3-D map of their location.

the robots could not gain traction on the stairs leading to the upper level. Their awkwardness in maneuvering around obstacles and turning corners also lessened their effectiveness. Finally, the power plant's thick concrete walls made wireless communication difficult. Gill Pratt, DARPA's program manager, was deeply disappointed. "The great lesson of Fukushima," he said, "is that disasters are often fast moving and [it is] difficult to predict events, where the window of time for effective intervention is small."

"MAY THE BEST ROBOT WIN"

Pratt was determined not to lose another opportunity to use robots effectively. A year after the catastrophe, the DARPA Robotics Challenge was announced. It consisted of three increasingly difficult contests over two years. The purpose was to spur research on robots that can operate with less human direction as they maneuver in environments too hazardous for humans. Universities or companies participating in the challenge could provide their own robots, or they could program a DARPA-supplied model, the Atlas, manufactured by Boston Dynamics.

A humanoid robot, Atlas walks upright and grasps objects in strong, well-developed hands. Its head is equipped with a double camera and a laser range finder to determine distances. Although the competition pitted Atlases against one another (as well as other robots), each team programmed its robot differently, with its own software. This programming made each robot unique.

The robots at the DARPA competition were not autonomous. They could not make decisions on their own and depended on their human operators, sometimes called robot drivers. Hidden in garages hundreds of feet away from the competition, the drivers interpreted the data that came to them from the robots' sensors. Then they told the robots what moves to make next. Step by step, they led the robots through different tasks. Some of the drivers, however, used programs that gave the robots leeway in figuring out how to complete a task. So the robots in some cases acted independently.

At the DARPA Robotics Challenge in 2015, robot competitors performed tasks that might be required in an emergency situation, such as closing a valve on a leaking gas pipe or clearing debris from a doorway.

Twenty-three teams entered robots in the final competition in the summer of 2015. Each robot had to perform these eight simple but vital tasks that might be required in an emergency situation:

1. Get in a vehicle and drive it to a designated location.
2. Leave the vehicle and walk across debris.
3. Remove obstacles from a doorway.
4. Open the door and enter the building.
5. Locate a leaking pipe and close its valve.
6. Reconnect a hose or cable.
7. Climb a ladder.
8. Lift a tool from the disaster site, use it to break through a concrete barrier, and walk through the opening.

"The new discovery we made here is that there's some incredible untapped affinity [kinship] between people and robots that we saw for the first time. . . . Ordinary people, not roboticists, felt this identity, sympathy, empathy for the robot."

—DARPA Robotics Challenge organizer Gill Pratt

Thousands of spectators turned out to witness the event in Pomona, California. "May the best robot win," became the audience mantra. Spectators cheered when robots performed well and groaned when they toppled to the ground.

For challenge organizer Gill Pratt, audience reaction was almost as instructive as the actual robotic performances. "The new discovery we made here is that there's some incredible untapped affinity [kinship] between people and robots that we saw for the first time today. Ordinary people, not roboticists, felt this identity, sympathy, empathy for the robot. . . . When the robot succeeded, they felt they succeeded. . . . I see potential for robots to connect with people and create a society where people actually feel better."

CARS WITHOUT DRIVERS

Development of autonomous vehicles (also called self-driving cars, or robot cars) is one of the most rapidly advancing and widely publicized areas of robotics. As early as 1964, author Isaac Asimov predicted the development of vehicles with "robot brains." Optimistically, he believed that cars bound for a specific location would "proceed there without interference by the slow reflexes of a human driver."

Asimov's idea then might have seemed like another implausible scenario from a science fiction writer, but driverless cars make sense for a number of reasons. Self-driving cars are often considered safer than human drivers since they do not get distracted or tired. Because they have sensors and computers to guide their movements, they use road space more efficiently than human drivers. For instance, while a human driver might be checking the car radio at a red light and not realize that the light has turned green until a few seconds later, a driverless car will begin moving immediately when the light changes. This kind of efficiency reduces traffic congestion. Fewer traffic jams can mean less car exhaust and air pollution. And driverless technology gives those who cannot drive themselves, such as some disabled and elderly people, more mobility and independence. It removes the hassles of having to arrange for rides from another person.

In the 1980s, researchers at Bundeswehr University Munich in Germany converted a Mercedes van into a self-driving vehicle and scientists at Carnegie Mellon University made over a Chevrolet van into a robot car. But little news about these projects filtered out to the public. Interest in autonomous cars perked up considerably at the start of the twenty-first century, when the US Congress directed the military to begin developing self-driving vehicles. The goal was to free soldiers in war zones from having to deliver supplies in hazardous areas, where they might encounter roadside bombs. Instead, driverless cars would do the job, and if they exploded, no drivers or passengers would be hurt. But the challenges were formidable, and military engineers made few advances.

To spur innovation, DARPA issued its first automotive Grand Challenge in 2002, inviting universities and corporations to compete in a 150-mile (241 km) driverless-car race. Fifteen vehicles participated in the event, held on March 13, 2004. The trek through the Mojave Desert in California included hazards and hardships similar to those a vehicle might face on a military mission in the Middle East, where US troops were by then fighting the Iraq War (2003–2011). Despite all the competitors' hard work, none of the vehicles even came close to finishing the course. Cars drove in circles, fell on their sides, became stuck in embankments, and caught on fire. But Tom Strat, deputy program manager of the event, believed it had achieved something positive. "One of the best ways to motivate engineers is

Guided by sensors and computers, driverless cars can identify other vehicles, road signs, traffic lights, pedestrians, and lane markers to navigate roadways. The device on the top of this self-driving car contains sensors that identify lane markers and the edges of roads. Other sensors are on the car's windshield, wheels, and front and side panels.

to tell them that there's something that can't be done," he said. "And what you saw today was people taking on that challenge and saying nah, it's not impossible, I'm [going to] try. Even though nobody got more than about 5 percent of the way through the course, this has made these engineers even more determined."

More than a decade later, Strat's words ring true. Two more DARPA challenges have done a great deal to stimulate interest in autonomous vehicles. Major automobile companies, including Volvo, Mercedes, Tesla, Audi, and Toyota, are investing huge sums to develop technologies for smart cars. One of the most talked-about players in the field is Google. Between 2009 and 2016, Google's self-driving cars drove more than 1.5 million miles (2.4 million km) in California, Arizona, Texas, and Washington State. State-of-the-art sensors (including lasers, cameras, and radar) and deep learning allow the cars to identify vehicles, road signs, intersections, and structures along roadways and to react to traffic, pedestrians, and road conditions. The technology is far from perfect, though. Rain, inadequately marked lanes, and the unpredictability of human drivers pose serious challenges to driverless cars.

On May 7, 2016, the first known fatality involving a driverless vehicle occurred in Florida. Joshua Brown was driving his Tesla Model S electric sedan, which can be driven manually or switched into autopilot (driverless) mode. Brown put the car on autopilot, and it failed to brake when a tractor-trailer turned in front of it. The car drove full speed into the trailer and crashed, killing Brown. Since then Tesla has announced plans to download new software into its cars. According to company chief Elon Musk, this software could have prevented the collision.

About four months after the accident, on September 20, 2016, the US Department of Transportation issued a fifteen-point safety checklist for autonomous vehicles. At the same time, President Barack Obama published an editorial in the *Pittsburgh Post-Gazette* hailing the advantages of self-driving cars and their "potential to save tens of thousands of lives each year." He also acknowledged the possibility of error. "Make no mistake," he declared, "if a self-driving car isn't safe, we have the authority to pull it off the road. We won't hesitate to protect the American public's safety."

THE FUTURE OF WARFARE: "ALL MANNER OF ROBOTS"

Safety is also the most important issue when it comes to military robots. On the battlefield, robots have the potential to save lives as well as to destroy them. In combat in the Middle East, the US military has used robots to disarm bombs and to carry out reconnaissance (searches) in areas that are too risky for soldiers. Unpiloted drones, operated by controllers on the ground, have conducted aerial bombing missions, sparing human pilots the danger of such attacks (while hitting targets on the ground). A robotics senior research scientist for the US Army, Robert Sadowski, hopes to see "robotics and autonomous systems [become] as ubiquitous [widespread] as apps on your cellphone and . . . viewed [by soldiers] as teammates rather than just a tool."

All military robots and AI are under human control—even if the human is many miles away. Concerned citizens of many nations would like to keep it that way. They find the idea of a machine making life-or-death decisions to be morally unacceptable. Despite such objections, some engineers are working on lethal autonomous weapons systems (LAWS). LAWS can act independently, even to the point of selecting and firing on targets. In fact, the Asian nation of South Korea may already be using such "killer robots." South Korea uses robots called SGR-A1s to patrol its border with North Korea. Armed with machine guns, these powerful robots have heat and light sensors that can detect humans within a 2-mile (3.2 km) range. Although distant humans control the robots, some military observers believe they may have the ability to open fire autonomously.

A 2015 report from the international organization Human Rights Watch and Harvard Law School urged the United Nations (an international humanitarian and peacekeeping group) to ban LAWS before they become a battlefield reality. No matter how carefully programmed, the arguments go, LAWS cannot understand the full context of any given situation. As machines, they cannot be held accountable for their actions. So who is to blame if an autonomous robot kills innocent victims? No nations have laws that hold manufacturers, computer programmers, or military commanders responsible for a robotic weapon's mistakes. According to Bonnie Docherty of Human Rights Watch, "No accountability means no deterrence [prevention] of future crimes, no retribution [justice] for victims, no social condemnation of the responsible party." As the prospect of true autonomous weapons draws closer, experts continue to debate if the weapons would take more lives than they saved.

Autonomous or not, robots are poised to change the face of warfare. Some experts predict that by 2040, every US soldier may be issued a personal robot. They say that when opposing armies confront each other, robots will be the first to enter the fray. "A time traveler from today," concludes a report issued by the US Army in 2015, "would be immediately taken with the 'over-crowding' of the battlefield of 2050 populated by all manner of robots, robots that greatly out-number human fighters."

ROBOTS IN SPACE

In space as well as on Earth, robots are expected to take over many responsibilities. From smart rovers exploring the surface of Mars to humanoid robots monitoring spacecraft, artificial intelligence has proved indispensable to space agencies worldwide. Several factors make robotic exploration extremely practical. Besides minimizing human risk, robots accumulate more significant data. For example, the rover *Curiosity*, which landed on Mars in 2012, not only gathers rocks and soil with its 7-foot (2.1 m) arm, but it also heats the samples and analyzes the gases they release. The results shed light on how the rocks and soils were formed. *Curiosity* is also testing the Martian soil for hydrogen (an element in water) and checking for organic substances (which contain carbon, a building block of life).

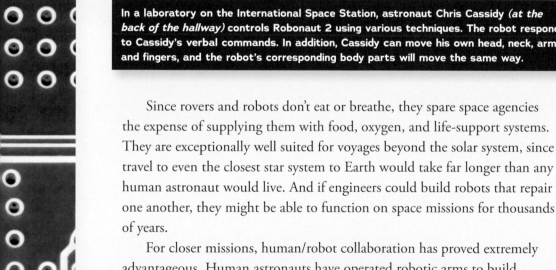

In a laboratory on the International Space Station, astronaut Chris Cassidy *(at the back of the hallway)* controls Robonaut 2 using various techniques. The robot responds to Cassidy's verbal commands. In addition, Cassidy can move his own head, neck, arms, and fingers, and the robot's corresponding body parts will move the same way.

Since rovers and robots don't eat or breathe, they spare space agencies the expense of supplying them with food, oxygen, and life-support systems. They are exceptionally well suited for voyages beyond the solar system, since travel to even the closest star system to Earth would take far longer than any human astronaut would live. And if engineers could build robots that repair one another, they might be able to function on space missions for thousands of years.

For closer missions, human/robot collaboration has proved extremely advantageous. Human astronauts have operated robotic arms to build, maintain, and repair the International Space Station (ISS), an orbiting research laboratory. In 2000 NASA produced Robonaut (a combination of the words *robot* and *astronaut*), a humanoid robot with nimble hands, capable of performing a variety of functions. The original Robonaut consisted of a torso attached to a fixed pedestal. Later, engineers attached the robot to wheels. In September 2014, Robonaut 2 (R2) achieved mobility when astronauts aboard the ISS gave it a pair of legs with sturdy clamps for feet. With legs, the robot can navigate the spacecraft on its own. The clamps on its feet allow it to latch onto objects and keep it from floating around the space station in zero gravity. R2 can also leave the station for space walks, sparing humans the danger of such an undertaking. With advanced vision technology, sensors, and artificial intelligence, R2 is able to move on its own, but astronauts can also control it remotely.

Robots even more advanced are in the works. Researchers at MIT and at Northeastern University in Boston are developing AI software to improve a robot called R5. Originally conceived as a disaster-relief robot, the 6-foot (1.8 m) 290-pound (132 kg) machine may one day travel to establish base camps on the moon and Mars to prepare for the arrival of human astronauts. Taskin Padir, lead researcher of the Northeastern team, will program R5 to exit an airlock hatch, climb down a ladder to a planetary surface, and collect soil samples. "Extreme space environments are dangerous for humans," he states. "And robots are ideal for dangerous tasks. . . . This is an effort to advance the autonomy of humanoid robots."

CHAPTER 6

SOCIALIZING WITH ROBOTS

Kismet, a wide-eyed robotic head, had an uncanny ability to follow and mimic human emotions. Developed in the late 1990s by MIT researcher Cynthia Breazeal, Kismet had giant eyes, floppy ears, and thick lips that all worked together to show happiness, sadness, surprise, anger, and even boredom. When no one spoke to it, the robot lowered its gaze, as if it were dejected or lonely. Sometimes a visitor to the lab would note Kismet's restlessness and wave a toy—perhaps a brightly colored ball—before its eyes. Kismet's expression then changed to register happiness. Encouraged, the visitor would continue the interaction, as if playing with a child.

But while Kismet's visitor experienced pleasure and amusement, was the robot really feeling anything? "Robots are not human, but humans are not the only things that have emotion," said Breazeal in 2007. "The question for robots is not, Will they ever have emotions? [The question is,] What are the emotions that are genuine for the robot?"

Breazeal's pioneering work in social robotics may help answer the question. Social robots work and interact with humans in everyday

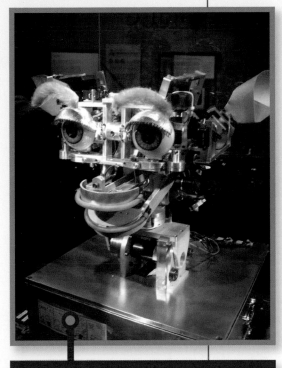

Kismet, a social robot built at MIT in the late 1990s, looks basic in comparison to modern-day social robots. But it showed that humans and robots could have meaningful interactions.

settings, but as Breazeal shows, they don't have to be humanoid or even mobile. Her latest creation, Jibo, unveiled in 2014 and billed as "the world's first family robot," looks more like a table lamp than a person. Consisting of a head with a round monitor; a small, sleek body; and a base, Jibo is designed to remain stationary on a countertop or table. His friendly voice (Breazeal refers to Jibo as "he"—not "it"), expressive screen, and ability to swivel and bend toward the person addressing him are designed to elicit feelings of trust and genuine fondness.

HAPPY DOGS

The four-legged robot AIBO (which means "companion" in Japanese and also stands for Artificial Intelligence roBOt) had a great deal in common with biological dogs. Sold by Sony Corporation to consumers between 1999 and 2006, AIBO could sense sights and sounds, learn, and demonstrate emotion. In return, the lucky human owners of AIBOs bonded strongly with their small, expressive robots. In 1998, before they were available for sale, AIBOs began playing soccer in the RoboCup competition. After scoring a goal, the robots would break into a happy dance to the delight of the audience. In 2006 AIBO was inducted into the Robot Hall of Fame at Carnegie Mellon University.

Two AIBO robots demonstrate their soccer skills at the Sony Computer Science Lab.

Among his many functions, Jibo can take photos at family gatherings and remind individuals of upcoming appointments. Even more promising, he has an open platform. That means that developers can create new apps for the robot the way they do for other electronic devices. But users get much more from Jibo than a variety of apps. "It's a warmer experience," Breazeal told the *Washington Post*, comparing Jibo to a smartphone or a computer screen. "[Jibo is] not this cold, kind of pure information-based persona." She views Jibo as a youthful, personable, and entertaining character.

Other manufacturers of social robots aim for similar positive images. Blue Frog Robotics's 2-foot-tall (0.6 m) mobile Buddy rolls around the house performing a variety of tasks. Its face consists of an Android operating system tablet, which its human "family" can use to program it. Another social robot, Pepper, is designed to respond to users' moods and to talk, gesture, and navigate on a wheeled base. Aldebaran Robotics, a French company, launched the vaguely humanoid robot in Japan in the summer of

2015. The price tag was $1,600 (198,000 Japanese yen) and $200 (24,600 yen) in monthly data and insurance fees. One thousand Peppers sold out in less than a minute.

BONDING WITH ROBOTS

Even robots not specially programmed to socialize can have strong effects on those around them—especially in critical situations. The PackBots manufactured by iRobot are designed solely for doing jobs, not for emotional bonding. But soldiers who have worked with PackBots that disable and dispose of bombs sometimes develop deep feelings for the

At a military base in Massachusetts, a US marine trains with a robot designed to carry heavy loads and cross tough terrain. Military personnel sometimes become emotionally attached to robots that work with them in dangerous situations.

SEEING DOUBLE

As a roboticist, Hiroshi Ishiguro understands the concept of the uncanny valley, but it has not stopped him from creating a robot that looks exactly like him. Ishiguro used silicon rubber to create natural-looking skin and even donated some of his own hair to his robotic double. Fixed permanently in a seated position, the remotely controlled robot mimics Ishiguro's tone of voice and head movements. Ishiguro refers to his double and other robots based on actual persons as Geminoids, from the Latin word *geminus*, which means "twin."

machines. Military men and women have even been known to risk their own safety to rescue a robot. They have gathered fragments of robots destroyed by bombs and tried to have them repaired. Soldiers have honored damaged or destroyed robots with unofficial military promotions, Purple Heart awards (given to soldiers who are wounded or killed in action), and military funerals.

According to Kate Darling, an MIT professor and expert in robot ethics, humans tend to anthropomorphize—to project human attributes onto any moving object, even something as featureless as a vacuum-cleaning Roomba. A more lifelike robot, such as Spot, a Boston Dynamics model built to resemble a dog, elicits an even greater response. In 2015 Boston Dynamics released a promotional video that showed a person kicking Spot. The point was to demonstrate the robot's ability to right itself after it stumbled and to keep going. Instead of seeing a well-constructed machine, however, many viewers saw an instance of animal abuse. They felt indignant on the robot's behalf and vented their anger on social media.

For social robots to fulfill their missions, humans have to feel comfortable interacting with them. For a successful interaction, appearance becomes very important. Research shows that a robot that bears a strong resemblance to a human and moves in a natural manner will elicit feelings of trust—but only up to a point. According to a theory known as the uncanny valley, when a robot begins to look too much like a human, users become uneasy. The idea that something so lifelike can be inanimate strikes people as creepy. Some researchers dismiss the uncanny valley, however. Roboticist David Hanson, who specializes in rubber-skinned, highly humanlike robot heads (he created the very lifelike Android Dick in 2005), has little use for the concept. "In my experience," he says, "people get used to [humanlike] robots very quickly. As in, within minutes."

"THESE ARE ROBOTS THAT PRETEND THEY LOVE YOU"

Critics of social robots are quick to point out the drawbacks of assigning a human personality to a machine. MIT psychologist Sherry Turkle is blunt in her assessment. "These are robots that pretend they love you, they pretend they have a life, they pretend they have friendship—this is a pretend relationship, and pretend empathy." She fears that those who develop an emotional reliance on machines might lose the desire and the ability to relate to real people in a meaningful way.

The concern about emotional links between humans and machines can be traced back to the mid-1960s, when MIT professor Joseph Weizenbaum developed a computer program known as Eliza. Named after a character in the musical *My Fair Lady*, his software allowed a person to have a seemingly normal text discussion with a computer. All Eliza was really doing, however, was turning its partner's statements into questions and picking up on certain key words. Here is a typical snippet of conversation:

Human: You are like my father in some ways.
Eliza: What resemblance do you see?
Human: You are not very aggressive but I think you don't want me
    to notice that.
Eliza: What makes you think I am not very aggressive?

Human: You don't argue with me.
Eliza: Why do you think I don't argue with you?

The conversations could be relatively straightforward or branch into strange and illogical byways. But despite its occasional glitches, Eliza was a big hit. Users knew it was a computer program, yet they related to Eliza as if it were a person, often confiding personal details about their lives. Weizenbaum was amazed and then deeply troubled that some would accept a shallow machine interaction as an alternative to more significant human conversation. "Since we do not now have ways of making computers wise," he wrote, "we ought not to give computers tasks that demand wisdom."

Fifty years after Eliza's creation, talking robots are still popular. Many take the form of computer programs that simulate human conversation. Responding by voice or text to users' questions, these chatbots can be found online, in messaging apps, or embedded in certain operating systems. For instance, Apple's well-known personal assistant Siri is a chatbot. Some businesses use chatbots to take telephone orders from customers or to handle customer service questions. Other individuals rely on chatbots to

AN OUTSTANDING TEACHER

As a teaching assistant for an online course at the Georgia Institute of Technology, Jill Watson responded to students' e-mails promptly. Watson helped them design computer programs, reminded them of due dates, and posted thought-provoking questions on the course website.

It wasn't until the end of the term that students learned the startling truth: Jill Watson was an artificial intelligence. Students were dumbfounded. Professor Ashok Goel, who had arranged with IBM to use Jill in his course on artificial intelligence, was pleased with Watson's performance. "Most chatbots operate at the level of a [beginner]," he explained. "Jill operates at the level of an expert."

keep their schedules, make their appointments, and provide them with information. According to Ted Livingston, founder of a mobile messaging service, "Chat apps will come to be thought of as the new browsers; [chat] bots will be the new websites; this is the beginning of a new Internet."

Advocates of social robots argue that the machines are not meant to replace human interactions but to enhance them. In fact, Cynthia Breazeal calls the social robot "an extender of our human capacity." She says that the United States and other countries don't have enough caretakers to assist the elderly or enough teachers to give children individual attention. Social robots could fill the void, helping senior citizens to live independently and interacting one-on-one with schoolchildren in busy classrooms.

Social robots could fill the void, helping senior citizens to live independently and interacting one-on-one with schoolchildren in busy classrooms.

Some researchers believe that children with autism, a condition that impairs communication skills, can benefit from therapy sessions with robots. Although autistic children can be withdrawn and frightened of social interactions, they tend to find dealing with robots less threatening than relating to other humans. A robot is usually smaller and less complex than a person. And it can be programmed to focus on one aspect of social behavior at a time. For example, if an autistic child finds it difficult to make eye contact with others, the robot can focus on this skill, helping the child look others in the eye during conversations and other social interactions.

SENTIENT ROBOTS?

Although social robots serve useful purposes—they astound, delight, and entertain—they are severely limited. They don't think or truly appreciate what's going on around them. And no robot comes close to interacting with a human in the same way another human does. For a machine to fully understand and completely communicate with people, it would have to have artificial general intelligence and the ability to think and feel in the same way humans do. No one knows when or if a robot or an AI platform might cross the line and become a sentient being. Some researchers believe this will never happen, but others think the phenomenon may be just around the corner.

CHAPTER 7

THE SINGULARITY

When Google hired AI researcher Ray Kurzweil to develop machine learning and language processing techniques, the artificial intelligence community took note. A futurist (one who tries to predict what life might be like in the future, based on current trends), Kurzweil has a habit of making predictions that come true. "In 1999, I said that in about a decade we would see technologies such as self-driving cars and mobile phones that could answer your questions, and people criticized these predictions as unrealistic," he told the press when his Google job was announced in December 2012. "Fast forward a decade—Google has demonstrated self-driving cars, and people are indeed asking questions of their Android phones."

Kurzweil's most daring predictions have to do with an even bigger issue—artificial general intelligence. Not only is he optimistic, but he is also quite specific in his pronouncements. Kurzweil believes that computers will have enough awareness to pass the Turing test by 2029. Their breadth of knowledge, he says, will allow machines to converse as coherently and naturally as humans do.

But Kurzweil sees this achievement as a mere stepping-stone on the road to superintelligence. In his view, machines will continue to improve, reprogramming themselves and downloading massive amounts of information from the Internet until they exceed human intelligence. Kurzweil predicts that this new reality, known as the Singularity, will occur in 2045. First coined by science fiction writer Vernor Vinge in 1993, Singularity describes a time when machines have surpassed humans in intelligence and become trillions of times more powerful than the computers of the early twenty-first century. Kurzweil envisions the Singularity as a transformed world in which machines will make us better and smarter and will prolong our lives indefinitely.

THE LAW OF ACCELERATING RETURNS

Kurzweil bases his predictions on what he calls the Law of Accelerating Returns, a variant of Moore's Law. Moore's Law is named for Gordon Moore, who cofounded the computer chip company Intel. In the 1960s, he observed that the transistors that controlled electric currents in computers were shrinking in size so fast that each year, twice as many could fit on a computer chip as the year before. Kurzweil's law applies this same doubling to the speed, memory, and power of computers.

AI PIONEER: RAY KURZWEIL

Long before Ray Kurzweil was thinking about the Singularity, he was an inventor of groundbreaking electronic devices. Growing up in New York City in the 1950s, Kurzweil learned computer science from an uncle. He created some of his first computer programs to help with his homework in high school. Kurzweil loved music and developed programs that analyzed the works of famous classical musicians and then created original compositions in similar styles. For this accomplishment, the fifteen-year-old received first place in the Westinghouse Science Talent Search and an invitation to visit the White House in 1963. A year later, he showed off his invention on the TV game show *I've Got a Secret*.

After graduation from MIT, Kurzweil began to market his inventions. He created a flatbed scanner and a machine that could convert written text into speech. Then he merged the two technologies into a machine that could read to the blind. In 1983 he created an electronic keyboard that impressed professional musicians. They could not tell the difference between the keyboard's synthesized sounds and those from real instruments.

AI expert Ray Kurzweil predicts that by the year 2045, computers will be smarter than humans.

In the 1990s, Kurzweil began considering the possible future of humanity. His motto "Live long enough to live forever" reflects his controversial belief that disease and death will be overcome in a post-Singularity world. "We will transcend all the limitations of our biology," he told the *New York Times* in 2010. "That is what it means to be human—to extend who we are."

Kurzweil often uses a simple fable, "The King's Chessboard," to illustrate what happens. To reward a wise man who had done him a great service, a king agreed to give him grains of rice that would be counted on a chessboard. The first square would hold one grain. The second square would hold double that, or two grains. The third square would hold double the previous amount, or four grains of rice. And so on until all sixty-four squares of the chessboard were filled. But if the king thought he was getting a bargain, he soon learned otherwise. The eighth square called for 128 grains of rice, too many to fit on a single square of the chessboard. As the amount kept doubling, the rice had to be delivered by the wagonload. And still the rice kept doubling for a grand total of more than 270 billion tons (245 billion metric tons) of rice. There was not enough rice in the kingdom to pay the wise man.

In the same way, electronic devices don't merely improve at a steady linear pace, advancing in a straightforward manner the way a person might walk at a constant rate toward a goal. Instead, electronics improve at a rate that is constantly doubling, with dizzying results, including a dramatic upsurge in computer intelligence. Such an exponential increase in computing ability is expected to lead to an "intelligence explosion," a phrase first used by mathematician I. J. Good in 1965. Once this occurs, Good speculated, "The intelligence of man would be left far behind." This is the point that Vinge and Kurzweil have dubbed the Singularity.

What will these developments mean for those who live through them? Some individuals, such as Kurzweil, have a positive vision in which humanity reaps multiple benefits from the growth in computer intelligence. Others, like physicist Stephen Hawking and Swedish philosopher Nick Bostrom, have grave misgivings about sharing Earth with entities more intelligent than we are.

UTOPIAN DREAM

Those who agree with Kurzweil view the Singularity as a gateway to a utopian dream. They envision a world of clean and abundant energy, an end to illness and poverty, a life free of suffering and tedious tasks, and

leisure to enjoy the many benefits of the new existence. They say that men and women will merge with artificial intelligence through brain and body implants, boosting health and strength. Kurzweil predicts that by the 2030s, humans will have become "more non-biological than biological," a condition sometimes known as transhumanism. Kurzweil and a group of like-minded individuals known as Singularitarians believe that ultimately, many humans will decide to abandon biology altogether by uploading their consciousness into computers. Their minds will live on without their bodies.

Ray Kurzweil predicts that by the 2030s, humans will have become "more non-biological than biological."

But the fulfillment of Kurzweil's controversial vision will require more than supersmart computers. Other technologies, such as genetic engineering (altering genes, the biological units that determine how living things grow and function), will also play important roles. Kurzweil says that techniques developed with the help of artificial intelligence will allow doctors to replace damaged genes with normal, healthy ones, "reprogram[ming] our biology," with the goal of eliminating disease and increasing human physical and mental capacities.

Kurzweil also believes that nanotechnology, the manipulation of infinitesimal (super-small) particles of matter, will combine with AI to transform human society. In Kurzweil's words, nanotechnology will "enable us to redesign and rebuild—molecule by molecule—our bodies and brains and the world with which we interact, going far beyond the limitations of human biology." He speculates that billions of nanobots (microscopic, semiautonomous machines) will course through the human bloodstream, killing disease-causing organisms, disposing of contaminants, and correcting mistakes in the genetic code. Kurzweil also thinks that nanobots will interact with neurons in the brain to greatly enhance human intelligence. In his scenario, we will be able to download information from the Internet directly into our brains. Even hearts will be rendered unnecessary because nanorobotic blood cells will circulate through the body under their own power, with no need for a heart to pump the blood.

In 2008 Kurzweil cofounded Singularity University in Silicon Valley. The school offers courses, conferences, and other programs to prepare people for leadership roles in the envisioned technological revolution.

"SUMMONING THE DEMON"

What would it be like to live in a world where humans are not the highest form of intelligence? The fact that no one knows what will happen is enough to alarm many. But physicist and AI researcher Stephen Omohundro, founder of Self-Aware Systems in Palo Alto, California, has some interesting speculations, which James Barrat summarizes in his book *Our Final Invention: Artificial Intelligence and the End of the Human Era*. Any self-improving, superintelligent machine, Omohundro reasons, will make achieving its goals its number one priority. He believes that these four overriding principles will govern its actions:

1. A superintelligence will be efficient, doing whatever it takes to meet its objectives in the quickest, most effective manner. This might include inventing new technologies and creating virtual environments in which to conduct experiments.
2. A superintelligence will take whatever measures are necessary to protect its existence. If humans pose a threat or a perceived threat, a superintelligence will find clever ways to defend itself, such as making numerous copies of itself and hiding them in computer clouds.
3. A superintelligence will go to great, almost unbelievable lengths to gain the resources it needs to complete its mission. Omohundro puts it bluntly: "These systems intrinsically [naturally] want more stuff. They want more matter, they want more free energy, they want more space, because they can meet their goals more effectively if they have those things." For instance, he thinks that a superintelligence might build

The United States and its allies use the MQ-9 Reaper, a military drone, to spy and drop bombs on enemy targets. Human operators control the Reaper, but someday drones equipped with advanced artificial intelligence might make their own decisions about bombing operations, a scenario that frightens many.

reactors to release nuclear energy from atoms. Or it might embark on space exploration to acquire more mineral resources.

4. A superintelligence will be creative; it will explore innovative methods to meet its goals as fully as possible. From a human standpoint, the machine might come up with some unexpected and disturbing consequences. James Barrat gives a hypothetical example in which a superintelligence programmed to protect humans decides to imprison them in their homes for their own safety.

Of course, such a scenario might never happen. Nevertheless, the example is a warning that superintelligence could lead to bizarre, totally unanticipated results.

MIT physics professor Max Tegmark is worried about the potential dangers of superintelligence. In April 2014, he hosted a gathering of thirty-three scientists and others to talk about the hazards of the new, rapidly progressing technologies. Their discussions led to the establishment of the

Future of Life Institute, an organization dedicated to researching and raising public awareness of the safety issues surrounding superintelligence.

Together with Nobel Prize–winning physicist Frank Wilczek, AI researcher Stuart Russell, and Stephen Hawking, Tegmark composed a letter that was published in the online newspaper the *Huffington Post*. "Success in creating AI would be the biggest event in human history," they wrote. "Unfortunately, it might also be the last, unless we learn how to avoid the risks. . . . Whereas the short-term impact of AI depends on who controls it, the long-term depends on whether it can be controlled at all." The risks, according to the writers, include "autonomous weapon systems that can choose and eliminate their own targets." By December 2015, the Future of Life Institute had awarded $7 million in grants for proposals on ways to minimize the dangers of AI.

Science fiction sometimes captures the danger of trusting AI too much. H.A.L. 9000, the eerily sentient computer from the iconic 1968 film *2001: A Space Odyssey*, had a will of its own. Claiming to be "foolproof and incapable of error," H.A.L. controlled most of the operations aboard the spaceship *Discovery One*. The problem came when H.A.L. wanted to take charge of the astronauts and the entire space mission as well. The supercomputer would stop at nothing—even murder—to get its way. In a heart-thumping cinematic sequence, the last astronaut left alive unplugs H.A.L.'s circuits one by one as the frightened computer begs him to stop.

Almost fifty years after the movie's release in 1968, scientists acknowledge that the development of a strong artificial intelligence would create potential hazards as well as benefits. Even Ray Kurzweil acknowledges that AGI "will remain a double-edged sword." Besides helping humankind, he observes, "it will also empower destructive ideologies [ideas]."

Speaking at MIT in 2014, Elon Musk, the founder of Tesla and the space exploration company SpaceX, is even more fearful. He cautioned, "With artificial intelligence, we are summoning the demon." Researchers aim to program computers with strong human values to prevent negative consequences and maximize the benefits to humanity.

CHAPTER 8

FRIENDLY, HOSTILE, OR INDIFFERENT?

Lieutenant Commander Data, the android whose intelligence dwarfs that of his crewmates on the television series *Star Trek: The Next Generation*, shared the human desire to control his own destiny. But did he have the legal right? Starfleet commander Bruce Maddox was determined to upload Data's consciousness into a computer and disassemble his body to see how his brain worked. So Data fought to establish his status as an individual rather than a piece of property. During a tension-filled hearing, Data was turned off to demonstrate that the android was only a machine.

Captain Jean-Luc Picard, however, knew Data as a friend and respected crewmate—not a mere machine. Acting as Data's lawyer, Picard argued that to consider any self-aware entity property was to treat it as a slave. Just as parents don't own their children, neither could Starfleet own Data.

First airing in February 1989, this highly rated episode was ahead of its time. But as computers and robots get smarter, the question of rights for artificial intelligence may become a hotly debated topic. After Picard's impassioned plea, the judge sided with Data. The android could not be forced to undergo a procedure against his will.

But what if an AI wants to vote, adopt a child, or sue the company that made it? Where do we draw the line between human rights and AI rights? Sentient machines may need to be protected from humans who would enslave them. But humans may need protection from supersmart machines that are indifferent to their well-being or from other humans who would use robots and AI unscrupulously.

AI versus IA

Data was designed to work *with* humans—not to replace them. Though lacking emotions, he got along well with his colleagues. No one felt threatened by his superior intellect or his irrefutable logic. Data had his place on the bridge of the *Enterprise*, and so did everyone else. His expertise enhanced the overall efficiency of the entire crew. But the android might have been devised differently. He (and perhaps a few other supersmart androids) might have been programmed to take total charge of voyages, leaving humans free to enjoy a luxurious space vacation.

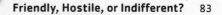

Often AI researchers face a decision similar to Data's fictional creators. Should artificially intelligent machines be designed to replace humans completely in a given situation? Or should machines be structured to supplement human capabilities and strengths, a position known as intelligence augmentation (IA)? In IA, robots would not be given the ability to act without human oversight. For instance, a computer designed to evaluate patients could not make a final diagnosis without the approval of a human physician.

In his book *Machines of Loving Grace*, John Markoff traces the tension between AI and IA to 1963, when two computer scientists formed research groups with very different aims. The Stanford Artificial Intelligence Center, founded by John McCarthy, wanted to create a "thinking machine" with general (human-level) intelligence. In contrast, Douglas Engelbart, who would later invent the computer mouse, explored computer systems that would augment, or boost, human intelligence, enabling workers to complete their jobs with more efficiency and speed. A dramatic example of augmented intelligence is the Google search engine, which provides a wealth of requested information for users to sort through and interpret as they see fit. An AGI system, on the other hand, might tell the person what information to search for and how it should be used.

TEACHING ETHICS TO ROBOTS

The possibility that computers might one day equal or surpass humans in intelligence raises the question of machine ethics. There's no guarantee that self-aware machines would think in the same way humans do or share human values. Researchers sometimes bring up Isaac Asimov's Three Laws of Robotics as a safeguard against machines harming humans. These laws are 1) a robot may not injure a human, 2) a robot must obey human orders unless they harm people, and 3) a robot must protect itself unless it breaks rules 1 and 2. But what works well in fiction may not protect us in real life.

Is it even possible to give robots a sense of ethics? Computer scientist Stuart Russell of the University of California–Berkeley thinks so.

In this scene from *2001: A Space Odyssey*, astronaut Dave Bowman unplugs H.A.L., the rogue computer that has already murdered his crewmates. Computers may become smarter than people in the future, but will they know right from wrong?

"As machines get smarter and smarter, it becomes more important that their goals, what they are trying to achieve with their decisions, are closely aligned with human values," he told the university's magazine. As with artificial intelligence itself, researchers might use two different methods to give morals to machines: the top-down approach and the bottom-up approach. In the first instance, scientists would program robots with the values they want the machines to have. Russell fears, however, that this technique might leave loopholes, since it wouldn't be possible to download every last ethical guideline into a computer. And humans often disagree about ethics. Ideas about right and wrong vary among those of different religions, different cultures, and different political parties. So the ethics programmed into a robot by one person might strike another person as objectionable.

The bottom-up approach is somewhat akin to machine learning, in which a robot or AI would gain its ethical knowledge from thousands of

"LIFE, LIBERTY, AND THE PURSUIT OF GREATER COGNITION"

When Peter Remine founded the American Society for the Prevention of Cruelty to Robots (ASPCR) in 1999, he knew the organization was ahead of its time. He knew that few people would take it seriously, and he saw the irony of what he was doing. "I just made a humorous website based on an idea that might someday actually become relevant," he told the online magazine *Motherboard*.

Still, Remine believes that if and when robots become self-aware, they will be entitled to certain basic rights. He states that these rights are "life, liberty and the pursuit of greater cognition [intellectual activity]." The list is a riff on the US Declaration of Independence, which declares that Americans have a right to life, liberty, and the pursuit of happiness.

examples. Instead of being programmed with rules and regulations, the robot would learn good behavior by observing individuals and copying what they did—for example, shaking hands as a greeting or helping someone who had fallen down.

In a related technique, called inverse reinforcement learning, the robot wouldn't merely copy actions. It would come to understand the motives behind them. Russell believes that with access to the inexhaustible amount of information in TV programs, news broadcasts, Internet postings, websites, movies, and books, robots could learn right from wrong. They "could learn what makes people happy, what makes them sad, what they do to get put in jail, what they do to win medals." To many, the very idea sounds absurd. And no twenty-first-century robot even comes close to distinguishing between right and wrong. But for a peaceful coexistence between humans and AGI, the machines would have to share our values.

DOOMSDAY OR A NEW DAWN?

Singularitarians predict that someday humans and machines will be able to merge—that we'll be able to upload our consciousnesses into computers. Others find the idea not only unrealistic but also unwelcome. Yale University computer scientist David Gelernter denies the validity of an uploaded consciousness. "What does that even mean?" he asked during a 2016 interview with *Time* magazine. "If my mind is running on another computer, it is no longer me." Gelernter believes that emotions and bodily sensations are essential to the creation of the human mind. "Consciousness," he declares, "is the work of the whole body"—not merely the brain. Furthermore, he says, consciousness not only changes throughout a person's lifetime but daily slides across a broad spectrum, from intense concentration (high end of the spectrum) to sleepiness (low end), with an indefinite number of states in between. To be human, asserts Gelernter, is to experience that full gamut, with all of its logic, memories, dreams, fears, joys, and longings. Our biology is part of what defines us. If humans become part machine, Gelernter believes, we will lose essential aspects of our consciousness and in fact forfeit our humanity.

Even if humans and machines remain distinct, Gelernter believes that machines will continue to get smarter and that eventually a machine will achieve the human-level intelligence quotient (IQ—a measure of intelligence) of 100. To date, no computer has come close to this level. But Gelernter says that once this milestone is achieved, it will only be a matter of time before machines achieve astronomical IQs of 500 and then 5,000. (Compare that to a brilliant human such as chess master Garry Kasparov, whose IQ is said to be above 190.) "We don't have the vaguest idea what an IQ of 5,000 would mean," Gelernter wrote in an essay for the *Wall Street Journal*. He speculates that in time, machines will be so smart that humans will not stand out to them in any meaningful way. They will not consider humans to be any more special than any other animal or even plants. And therefore, they will have no regard for our well-being. "Robots with superhuman intelligence," Gelernter cautions, "are as dangerous, potentially, as nuclear bombs."

A robot named Nao shows how intelligent machines can help humankind. Here, Nao acts as a stand-in for a boy hospitalized with leukemia. The boy remotely controls Nao from his hospital room, using a tablet computer. Nao's sensors allow the boy to see and hear what's happening in the classroom and to participate in lessons along with the other students.

Although no one can predict how superintelligence will develop and what its motives might be, some researchers prefer to emphasize the positive rather than dwell on what could go wrong. Charles Ortiz, head of AI at the software company Nuance Communications, believes that artificial general intelligence won't arrive for many years. And when it does, "I don't see any reason to think that as machines become more intelligent . . . they would want to destroy us or do harm," he said in 2014. He thinks that smart machines might even feel indebted to their human creators, speculating that they might become "our teachers" or "our colleagues." While acknowledging the possibility that AI might harm us or that unscrupulous humans might misuse AI for their own ends, Ortiz says that "doomsday scenarios" are overblown. "The emphasis should instead be on the good that can come out of AI: AI products do not need warning labels."

ONGOING DEBATE

The arguments are certain to continue. Will AGI and superintelligence be friendly, hostile, or indifferent to us? What can experts do to ensure a positive outcome? The ongoing public debate seeks to prepare the world for the inevitable technological changes and to spur AI researchers to explore the economic, social, and safety implications of their work.

Humans are still the smartest entities on the planet and are likely to remain so for a long time. But computers already have an almost unlimited capacity to sift through data and to rapidly solve problems that would take humans months—or even years—to work out. As our partners, intelligent machines have much to teach us about the world—and even ourselves. By studying artificial intelligence and how it differs from us, we can learn more about what makes us human.

The passenger van Olli, which takes riders through the streets of Washington, DC, includes two kinds of AI. First, Olli operates on self-driving vehicle technology. In addition, passengers on Olli can carry on conversations with IBM's Watson.

Hello. I'm

olli

I'm self-driving.
I'm adaptable.
I'm efficient, and
I'm around the corr

AT LOCAL MOT

A GLIMPSE OF THE FUTURE

The future of AI has come to Washington, DC. There, using a smartphone app, passengers can hail a 3D-printed, self-driving bus named Olli. The twelve-seater transports riders within the city limits at a top speed of about 8 miles (13 km) per hour. It also provides a voice interface through which passengers can talk to IBM's Watson about their route and about how Olli works.

Since toppling the two greatest *Jeopardy!* champions of all time and winning $1 million, Watson has been devouring millions of medical and legal documents and gaining new skills. With a knowledge base much broader than any doctor's or lawyer's, the robot can help diagnose a patient's illness or find relevant information about a court case. A special Watson app called Sophie keeps veterinarians current on the most recent treatments of animal diseases. Usher, another Watson app, allows visitors to enjoy personalized, interactive tours of museums. Watson has even trained with the Institute of Culinary Education in New York City and created sixty-five original recipes. Its book *Cognitive Cooking with Chef Watson* was published in 2015. And thanks to IBM's acquisition of 140,000 weather forecasting stations, along with data from the US National Weather Service and weather stations around the world, Watson will soon be making forecasts more accurate than ever.

> **"It's hard to think of a job that a computer ultimately won't be able to do as well [as] if not better than we can do."**
>
> **—AI expert Toby Walsh**

Watson's achievements are only a small sampling of what advanced artificial intelligence will be able to accomplish. According to Toby Walsh, a world-renowned expert in AI, "It's hard to think of a job that a computer ultimately won't be able to do as well [as] if not better than we can do." Whether or not machines ever attain sentience, artificial intelligence will continue to revolutionize the way we live and work in ways we can scarcely imagine.

Source Notes

5   Tom Lamont, "Meet Watson, the Computer Set to Outsmart the Champions of *Jeopardy!*," *Guardian* (US ed.), February 5, 2011, http://www.theguardian.com/technology/2011 /feb/06/watson-ibm-computer-jeopardy-compete.

6   "I, for One Welcome Our New Computer Overlords," *Seeker*, February 17, 2011, http:// www.seeker.com/i-for-one-welcome-our-new-computer-overlords-1765179390.html.

8   Stephen Hawking, Stuart Russell, Max Tegmark, and Frank Wilczek, "Transcending Complacency on Superintelligent Machines," *Huffington Post*, last modified April 19, 2014, http://www.huffingtonpost.com/stephen-hawking/artificial-intelligence_b_5174265 .html.

9   Hector J. Levesque, *Thinking as Computation: A First Course* (Cambridge, MA: MIT Press, 2012), 3.

12 Kavita Iyer, "AI Robot Tells Human Creators That It Will Keep Them in a People Zoo," *TechWorm*, September 1, 2015, http://www.techworm.net/2015/09/ai-robot-tells-human -creators-that-it-will-keep-them-in-a-people-zoo.html.

14 "The Babbage Engine," Computer History Museum, accessed October 24, 2016, http:// www.computerhistory.org/babbage/overview/.

19 C. Dianne Martin, "ENIAC: The Press Conference That Shook the World," George Washington University, accessed October 24, 2016, https://www.seas.gwu.edu/~mfeldman /csci110/summer08/eniac2.pdf.

21 Luke Muehlhauser, "Introduction to Artificial Intelligence," *Common Sense Atheism*, March 8, 2011, http://commonsenseatheism.com/?p=13971.

21 Harry Henderson, *Artificial Intelligence: Mirrors for the Mind* (New York: Chelsea House, 2007), 33.

21 Pamela McCorduck, *Machines Who Think: A Personal Inquiry into the History and Prospects of Artificial Intelligence* (Natick, MA: A. K. Peters, 2004), 115.

22 John Markoff, *Machines of Loving Grace: The Quest for Common Ground between Humans and Robots* (New York: Ecco, 2015), 108.

22 Nick Bostrom, *Superintelligence: Paths, Dangers, Strategies* (Oxford: Oxford University Press, 2014), 5.

22 Henderson, *Artificial Intelligence*, 42.

22 Ibid., 53.

24 "Shakey," SRI International, accessed September 16, 2016, http://www.ai.sri.com/shakey/.

25 David Szondy, "Fifty Years of Shakey, the 'World's First Electronic Person,'" *New Atlas*, June 17, 2015, http://newatlas.com/shakey-robot-sri-fiftieth-anniversary/37668/.

27–28 Michael Schrage, "Fifth Generation Spurs a Global Computer Race," *Washington Post*, July 12, 1984, https://www.washingtonpost.com/archive/business/1984/07/12/5th-generation -spurs-a-global-computer-race/bbaebc1a-19d5-4b2d-9ba7-7f676849b1dc/.

28 "Sir Timothy Berners-Lee," Academy of Achievement, accessed February 24, 2017, http://prodloadbalancer-1055872027.us-east-1.elb.amazonaws.com/autodoc/page/ber1int-3.

33 Adam Rogers, "We Asked a Robot to Write an Obit for AI Pioneer Marvin Minsky," *Wired*, January 26, 2016, https://www.wired.com/2016/01/we-asked-a-robot-to-write-an-obit-for-ai-pioneer-marvin-minsky/.

34 Gary Marcus, "Is 'Deep Learning' a Revolution in Artificial Intelligence?," *New Yorker*, November 25, 2012, http://www.newyorker.com/news/news-desk/is-deep-learning-a-revolution-in-artificial-intelligence.

34 McCorduck, *Machines Who Think*, 105.

35 Markoff, *Machines of Loving Grace*, 144.

35 Ibid., 145.

35 Ibid., 147.

38 Adrian Lee, "The Meaning of AlphaGo, the AI Program That Beat a Go Champ," *MacLean's*, March 18, 2016, http://www.macleans.ca/society/science/the-meaning-of-alphago-the-ai-program-that-beat-a-go-champ/.

39 John Markoff, "Scientists See Promise in Deep-Learning Programs," *New York Times*, November 23, 2012, http://www.nytimes.com/2012/11/24/science/scientists-see-advances-in-deep-learning-a-part-of-artificial-intelligence.html.

39 Daniela Hernandez, "Meet the Man Google Hired to Make AI a Reality," *Wired*, January 16, 2014, http://www.wired.com/2014/01/geoffrey-hinton-deep-learning/.

42 "Danger Will Robinson Danger—*Lost in Space*," YouTube, 0:31, posted by "timtomp," April 19, 2009, https://www.youtube.com/watch?v=RG0ochx16Dg.

42 Ana Matronic, *Robot Universe: Legendary Automatons and Androids from the Ancient World to the Distant Future* (New York: Sterling, 2015), 105.

42 Ibid., 45.

44 Bill Condie, "Baxter's Young Brother Sawyer Brings Finesse to Industrial Robotics," *Cosmos*, April 27, 2015, https://cosmosmagazine.com/technology/baxter-s-younger-brother-sawyer-brings-finesse-to-industrial-robotics.

46 Erik Brynjolfsson and Andrew McAfee, *The Second Machine Age: Work, Progress, and Prosperity in a Time of Brilliant Technologies* (New York: W. W. Norton, 2014), 32.

47 David Bernard, "A Robot to Care for You in Old Age," *US News & World Report*, June 6, 2014, http://money.usnews.com/money/blogs/on-retirement/2014/06/05/a-robot-to-care-for-you-in-old-age.

48 Marina Koren, "How Raven, the Open-Source Surgical Robot, Could Change Medicine," *Popular Mechanics*, February 28, 2012, http://www.popularmechanics.com/science/health/a7470/how-raven-the-smart-robotic-helper-is-changing-surgery/.

49 Shahien Nasiripour, "White House Predicts Robots May Take Over Many Jobs That Pay $20 per Hour," *Huffington Post*, February 24, 2016, http://www.huffingtonpost.com/entry/white-house-robot-workers_us_56cdd89ce4b0928f5a6de955.

49   "Study—Robots Are Not Taking Jobs," Robotenomics, accessed October 24, 2016, https://robotenomics.com/2015/09/16/study-robots-are-not-taking-jobs/.

49   Steve Crowe, "Robots Not a Threat to Jobs: Rodney Brooks," *Robotics Trends*, July 29, 2016, http://www.roboticstrends.com/article/robots_not_a_threat_to_jobs_rodney_brooks.

51   John D. Sutter, "How 9/11 Inspired a New Era of Robotics," *CNN*, September 7, 2011, http://www.cnn.com/2011/TECH/innovation/09/07/911.robots.disaster.response/.

52   Ibid.

53   Eric Niller, "Robots Are Getting Closer to Having Humanlike Abilities and Senses," *Washington Post*, August 5, 2013, https://www.washingtonpost.com/national/health-science/robots-are-getting-closer-to-having-humanlike-abilities-and-senses/2013/08/05/61cb3cdc-8d9d-11e2-9838-d62f083ba93f_story.html.

54   Timothy Hornyak, "How Robots Are Becoming Critical Players in Nuclear Disaster Cleanup," *Science*, March 3, 2016, http://www.sciencemag.org/news/2016/03/how-robots-are-becoming-critical-players-nuclear-disaster-cleanup.

56   "Three Teams Take Top Honors at DARPA Robotics Challenge Finals," DARPA, June 7, 2015, http://www.darpa.mil/news-events/2015-06-06a.

56   Evan Ackerman and Enrico Guizzo, "DARPA Robotics Challenge: Amazing Moments, Lessons Learned, and What's Next," *IEEE Spectrum*, June 11, 2015, http://spectrum.ieee.org/automaton/robotics/humanoids/darpa-robotics-challenge-amazing-moments-lessons-learned-whats-next.

56   Ibid.

56   Ian Bogost, "The Secret History of the Robot Car," *Atlantic*, November 2014, http://www.theatlantic.com/magazine/archive/2014/11/the-secret-history-of-the-robot-car/380791/.

57–58   Marsha Walton, "Robots Fail to Complete Grand Challenge," *CNN*, March 6, 2004, http://www.cnn.com/2004/TECH/ptech/03/14/darpa.race/.

59   Barack Obama, "Barack Obama: Self-Driving, Yes, But Also Safe," *Pittsburgh Post-Gazette*, September 19, 2016, http://www.post-gazette.com/opinion/Op-Ed/2016/09/19/Barack-Obama-Self-driving-yes-but-also-safe/stories/201609200027.

59   George Seffers, "Robotic Systems May Take a Bullet for Soldiers," *Signal*, July 1, 2016, http://www.afcea.org/content/?q=Article-robotic-systems-may-take-bullet-soldiers.

60   Russell Christian, "The 'Killer Robots' Accountability Gap," Human Rights Watch, April 8, 2015, https://www.hrw.org/news/2015/04/08/killer-robots-accountability-gap.

60   Franz-Stefan Gady, "Super Humans and Killer Robots: How the US Army Envisions Warfare in 2050," *Diplomat*, July 24, 2015, http://thediplomat.com/2015/07/super-humans-and-killer-robots-how-the-us-army-envisions-warfare-in-2050/.

61   Markoff, *Machines of Loving Grace*, 117.

63   Tomasz Nowakowski, "NASA Counting on Humanoid Robots in Deep Space Exploration," Phys.org, January 26, 2016, http://phys.org/news/2016-01-nasa-humanoid-robots-deep-space.html.

65 Robin Marantz Henig, "The Real Transformers," *New York Times Magazine*, July 29, 2007, http://www.nytimes.com/2007/07/29/magazine/29robots-t.html?_r=0.

65 "Meet Jibo," Jibo, accessed October 31, 2016, https://www.jibo.com.

67 Joel Achenbach, "Social Robots: The Solution to Our Onscreen Addictions, or Just More Digital Weirdness?," *Washington Post*, December 28, 2015, https://www.washingtonpost.com/news/speaking-of-science/wp/2015/12/28/social-robots-the-solution-to-our-screen-addiction-or-more-digital-weirdness/.

70 Erik Sofge, "The Truth about Robots and the Uncanny Valley," *Popular Mechanics*, January 20, 2010, http://www.popularmechanics.com/technology/robots/a5001/4343054/.

70 Joel Achenbach, "AI Anxiety," *Washington Post*, December 27, 2015, http://www.washingtonpost.com/sf/national/2015/12/27/aianxiety/.

70–71 Joseph Weizenbaum, "ELIZA: A Computer Program for the Study of Natural Language Communication between Man and Machine," *Communications of the ACM* 9, no. 1 (January 1966): 35–36.

71 Henderson, *Artificial Intelligence*, 127.

71 Melissa Korn, "Imagine Discovering That Your Teaching Assistant Really Is a Robot," *Wall Street Journal*, May 6, 2016, http://www.wsj.com/articles/if-your-teacher-sounds-like-a-robot-you-might-be-on-to-something-1462546621.

72 Alexis Boncy, "Rise of the Chatbots," *Week*, April 14, 2016, http://theweek.com/articles/617833/rise-chatbots.

72 Alexandra Wolfe, "Cynthia Breazeal's Robotic Quest," *Wall Street Journal*, January 29, 2016, http://www.wsj.com/articles/cynthia-breazeals-robotic-quest-1454094777.

74–75 Neal Ungerleider, "Ray Kurzweil Now on the Job at Google," *Fast Company*, December 17, 2012, http://www.fastcompany.com/3004071/ray-kurzweil-now-job-google.

76 Henderson, *Artificial Intelligence*, 159.

76 Ashlee Vance, "Merely Human? That's So Yesterday," *New York Times*, June 12, 2010, http://www.nytimes.com/2010/06/13/business/13sing.html?pagewanted=all&_r=0.

77 James Barrat, *Our Final Invention: Artificial Intelligence and the End of the Human Era* (New York: Thomas Dunne Books, 2013), 104.

78 Bill Detwiler, "Kurzweil: Humans Will Be More Machine Than Biological by the 2030s," *Tech Republic*, July 16, 2008, http://www.techrepublic.com/blog/tr-dojo/kurzweil-humans-will-be-more-machine-than-biological-by-the-2030s/.

78 Ibid.

78 Ray Kurzweil, *The Singularity Is Near: When Humans Transcend Biology* (New York: Penguin Books, 2005), 260.

78 Ray Kurzweil, "GNR: The Building Blocks of the Singularity," Singularity and Nutrition, accessed October 24, 2016, https://sites.google.com/site/singularityandnutrition/gnr-the-building-blocks-of-the-singularity.

79 Barrat, *Our Final Invention*, 86.

81 Hawking, Russell, Tegmark, and Wilczek, "Transcending Complacency."

81 Ibid.

81 "2001: A Space Odyssey quotes," IMDb, accessed February 24, 2017, http://www.imdb
   .com/title/tt0062622/quotes.

81 Kurzweil, *Singularity Is Near*, 424.

81 Achenbach, "AI Anxiety."

85 Coby McDonald, "The Good, the Bad, and the Robot: Experts Are Trying to Make
   Machines Be 'Moral,'" *California Magazine*, June 4, 2015, http://alumni.berkeley.edu
   /california-magazine/just-in/2015-06-08/good-bad-and-robot-experts-are-trying-make
   -machines-be-moral.

86 Ibid.

86 Brian Anderson, "This Guy Wants to Save Robots from Abusive Humans," *Motherboard*,
   October 27, 2012, http://motherboard.vice.com/read/the-plan-to-protect-robots-from
   -human-cruelty.

86 Ibid.

87 Cubie King and David Von Drehle, "Encounters with the Arch-Genius, David Gelernter,"
   Time, February 25, 2016, http://time.com/4236974/encounters-with-the-archgenius/.

87 Ibid.

87 David Gelernter, "Machines That Will Think and Feel," *Wall Street Journal*, March 18,
   2016, http://www.wsj.com/articles/when-machines-think-and-feel-1458311760.

87 Ibid.

88 Tanya Lewis, "Artificial Intelligence: Friendly or Frightening?," *Live Science*, December 4,
   2014, http://www.livescience.com/49009-future-of-artificial-intelligence.html.

88 Charles Ortiz, "No AI Warning Label Necessary," *Tech Crunch*, April 13, 2015, https://
   techcrunch.com/2015/04/13/no-ai-warning-label-necessary/.

89 Ibid.

91 Guia Marie Del Prado, "Eighteen Artificial Intelligence Researchers Reveal the Profound
   Changes Coming to Our Lives," *Tech Insider*, October 26, 2015, http://www.techinsider
   .io/researchers-predictions-future-artificial-intelligence-2015-10.

91 Ibid.

Glossary

algorithm: a set of procedures or rules used by a computer in solving a problem

android: a mobile robot that usually resembles a human being

artificial general intelligence (AGI): a "thinking machine" that's able to learn on its own, modify its own programs, and solve the same kinds of problems that humans can solve, without human input

artificial intelligence: machinery with the ability to reason and solve problems. The term *artificial intelligence* also refers to the branch of computer science that deals with intelligent machines.

autonomous: capable of acting independently, without outside control. Autonomous machines can determine what actions to take without human direction.

chatbot: a computer program that can simulate human conversation. Examples include personal assistants such as Siri and chatbots that answer customers' questions on company websites.

deep learning: a process in which multilayered neural networks are exposed to vast amounts of data. On their own, the networks learn to analyze the data and draw conclusions.

drone: an unpiloted aircraft or ship, guided by remote control

expert systems: computers that store vast amounts of information about a specific field, such as business or medicine. Expert systems are also programmed with detailed rules about how to process this data.

intelligence augmentation: supplementing human intelligence with artificial intelligence rather than replacing human intelligence with artificial intelligence

Law of Accelerating Returns: a theory by Ray Kurzweil that electronic development—such as improvement in the speed, memory, and power of computers—proceeds at a rate that is continuously doubling

nanotechnology: the production and use of machines that are only slightly larger than atoms and molecules. Some researchers believe that AI will combine with nanotechnology to transform medicine and other disciplines.

neural nets: computer systems that loosely mimic the workings of the human brain

processor: a device that organizes information and directs the workings of a computer

robot: a machine that automatically performs complicated and often repetitive tasks. Many robots are designed to look like humans.

sentient: capable of thinking and feeling; being aware of one's existence

Singularity: a time in the future when machines will surpass humans in intelligence. Some researchers believe the Singularity will begin in 2045.

social robotics: the study of how robots and humans learn to relate to each other

strong artificial intelligence: an artificial intelligence that can understand and solve any problem that a human can

Turing test: a test in which a machine attempts to prove its intelligence by convincing an unseen conversational partner that it is human

weak artificial intelligence: an artificial intelligence that is narrowly tailored to do a specific task, such as conducting a computer search or analyzing a chemical compound

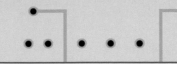

Selected Bibliography

Armstrong, Stuart. *Smarter Than Us: The Rise of Machine Intelligence*. Berkeley, CA: Machine Intelligence Research Institute, 2014.

Barrat, James. *Our Final Invention: Artificial Intelligence and the End of the Human Era*. New York: Thomas Dunne Books, 2013.

Bostrom, Nick. *Superintelligence: Paths, Dangers, Strategies*. Oxford: Oxford University Press, 2014.

Brooks, Rodney, Ray Kurzweil, and David Gelernter. "Gelernter, Kurzweil Debate Machine Consciousness." *Kurzweil Accelerating Intelligence*, December 6, 2006. http://www.kurzweilai.net/gelernter-kurzweil-debate-machine-consciousness-2.

Brynjolfsson, Erik, and Andrew McAfee. *The Second Machine Age: Work, Progress, and Prosperity in a Time of Brilliant Technologies*. New York: W. W. Norton, 2014.

Carr, Nicholas. *The Shallows: What the Internet Is Doing to Our Brains*. New York: W. W. Norton, 2010.

Chace, Calum. *Surviving AI: The Promise and Peril of Artificial Intelligence*. San Mateo, CA: Three Cs, 2015.

Ford, Martin. *Rise of the Robots: Technology and the Threat of a Jobless Future*. New York: Basic Books, 2015.

Gelernter, David. *The Tides of Mind: Uncovering the Spectrum of Consciousness*. New York: Liveright, 2016.

Goodell, Jeff. "Inside the Artificial Intelligence Revolution: A Special Report, Pt. 1." *Rolling Stone*, February 29, 2016. http://www.rollingstone.com/culture/features/inside-the-artificial-intelligence-revolution-a-special-report-pt-1-20160229.

———. "Inside the Artificial Intelligence Revolution: A Special Report, Pt. 2." *Rolling Stone*, March 9, 2016. http://www.rollingstone.com/culture/features/inside-the-artificial-intelligence-revolution-a-special-report-pt-2-20160309.

Joy, Bill. "Why the Future Doesn't Need Us." *Wired*, April 1, 2000. http://www.wired.com/2000/04/joy-2/.

Kurzweil, Ray. *The Singularity Is Near: When Humans Transcend Biology*. New York: Penguin Books, 2005.

Markoff, John. *Machines of Loving Grace: The Quest for Common Ground between Humans and Robots*. New York: Ecco, 2015.

———. "The Transhuman Condition." *Harper's*, August 2015. http://harpers.org/archive/2015/08/the-transhuman-condition/.

McCorduck, Pamela. *Machines Who Think: A Personal Inquiry into the History and Prospects of Artificial Intelligence*. Natick, MA: A. K. Peters, 2004.

Mindell, David A. *Our Robots, Ourselves: Robotics and the Myths of Autonomy*. New York: Viking, 2015.

Nocks, Lisa. *The Robot: The Life Story of a Technology*. Baltimore: Johns Hopkins University Press, 2007.

Whitby, Blay. *Artificial Intelligence: A Beginner's Guide*. Oxford: Oneworld, 2003.

FURTHER INFORMATION

Books

Brown, Jordan D. *Robo World: The Story of Robot Designer Cynthia Breazeal*. Washington, DC: Joseph Henry, 2006.

Ceceri, Kathy. *Robotics: Discover the Science and Technology of the Future with 20 Projects*. White River Junction, VT: Nomad, 2012.

Dufty, David. *How to Build an Android: The True Story of Philip K. Dick's Robotic Resurrection*. New York: Picador, 2013.

Goldstein, Margaret J., and Martin Gitlin. *Cyber Attack*. Minneapolis: Twenty-First Century Books, 2015.

Greenberger, Robert, and Sandra Giddens. *Careers in Artificial Intelligence*. New York: Rosen, 2007.

Henderson, Harry. *Artificial Intelligence: Mirrors for the Mind*. New York: Chelsea House, 2007.

January, Brendan. *Information Insecurity: Privacy under Siege*. Minneapolis: Twenty-First Century Books, 2016.

Kaplan, Jerry. *Humans Need Not Apply: A Guide to Wealth and Work in the Age of Artificial Intelligence*. New Haven: Yale University Press, 2015.

Karam, P. Andrew. *Artificial Intelligence*. New York: Chelsea House, 2012.

Kurzweil, Ray. *How to Create a Mind: The Secret of Human Thought Revealed*. New York: Penguin, 2013.

Leider, Rick. *Robots: Explore the World of Robots and How They Work for Us*. New York: Sky Pony, 2015.

Matronic, Ana. *Robot Universe: Legendary Automatons and Androids from the Ancient World to the Distant Future*. New York: Sterling, 2015.

Films

Ex Machina. DVD. Universal City, CA: Universal Pictures, 2015. In this big-screen thriller, a computer programmer takes part in a Turing test. He must evaluate the capabilities and consciousness of an artificial intelligence designed to look and act like a woman.

Her. DVD. Los Angeles: Annapurna Pictures, 2013. The lead character in this fictional film falls in love with an AI, a scenario that's not too far-fetched in an age of increasingly intelligent and lifelike machines.

Lo and Behold: Reveries of the Connected World. DVD. Venice, CA: Saville Productions, 2016. In this documentary, award-winning filmmaker Werner Herzog explores the future of artificial intelligence, robots, and their potential effects on human society.

Smartest Machine on Earth. DVD. Boston: WGBH Educational Foundation, 2011. This documentary introduces Watson in the run-up to its much-heralded match against Ken Jennings and Brad Rutter on *Jeopardy!* The filmmakers show what it takes to build a machine like Watson and where artificial intelligence might be headed.

2001: A Space Odyssey. DVD. Beverly Hills, CA: Metro-Goldwyn-Mayer, 1968. This science fiction classic features the intelligent computer H.A.L. 9000, which turns murderous toward its human colleagues during a mission to Jupiter.

Wounds of Waziristan. DVD. New York: Madiha Tahir and Parergon Films, 2013. This documentary film tells how US military drones sometimes accidentally kill and wound civilians. Humans control the drones, but the future might bring intelligent drones that can choose their own targets.

Websites

AITopics
http://aitopics.org
This comprehensive site maintained by the Association for the Advancement of Artificial Intelligence (AAAI) covers topics including AI history, AI in the news, games and puzzles, science fiction, robots, and much more.

IBM Watson
http://www.ibm.com/watson/
This site includes information on how IBM's Watson learns and answers questions. It also offers a video describing what the future may hold for Watson.

Robo Brain
http://robobrain.me/#/
Created by scientists at Cornell University in New York, Robo Brain helps robots deal with everyday tasks, such as opening a drawer or putting a garment onto a

hanger. At this website, Robo Brain introduces itself, explains how it learns, and presents some of the concepts it's learned recently.

Robot Hall of Fame

http://www.robothalloffame.org/inductees.html
Carnegie Mellon's Robot Hall of Fame includes both real robots, such as Shakey and BigDog, and fictional ones, such as Lieutenant Commander Data of *Star Trek: The Next Generation*. You can learn about them and other robots by visiting this site.

Robotics: Facts

http://idahoptv.org/sciencetrek/topics/robots/facts.cfm
This website from Idaho Public Television presents straightforward material on robotics, nanobots, and artificial intelligence. Illustrated with cartoons, it includes links to games, frequently asked questions, videos, and a glossary.

Robots for Kids

http://www.sciencekids.co.nz/robots.html
Here you can find games, projects, quizzes, and experiments about robots, plus articles about the history of robotics and different types of robots.

What Is Artificial Intelligence?

https://www.kidscodecs.com/what-is-artificial-intelligence/
This website from the online and print magazine *Kids, Code, and Computer Science* discusses the uses of AI and its potential for good as well as harm. Links to other articles on AI are included.

What Is Artificial Intelligence?

http://www.pitara.com/science-for-kids/5ws-and-h/what-is-artificial-intelligence/
This website from the Pitara Kids Network, includes easily accessible information on neural networks and the Turing test.

INDEX

Photo Acknowledgments

The images in this book are used with the permission of: © iStockphoto.com/standret (circuit board design); © iStockphoto.com/iLexx, p. 4; AP Photo/Seth Wenig, p. 5; REUTERS/Maxim Zmeyev, p. 10; REUTERS/John Gress, p. 12; © Harper's new monthly magazine/Volume 30, Issue 175, p. 34/Wikimedia Commons (public domain), p. 13; Library of Congress (LC-USZ62-45687), p. 15; © The Ada Picture Gallery/Wikimedia Commons (Public Domain), p. 16; The Granger Collection, New York, p. 18; © Time & Life Pictures/The LIFE Images Collection/Getty Images, p. 20; © Doug Wilson/CORBIS/Getty Images, p. 26; © TIMOTHY A. CLARY/AFP/Getty Images, p. 27; © iStockphoto.com/alengo, p. 30; © Jim Wilson/The New York Times/Redux, p. 31; © Frederic Lewis/Getty Images, p. 32; © Dan McCoy/Rainbow/SuperStock, p. 33; © Google/Getty Images, p. 38; Photo Researchers/Alamy Stock Photo, p. 41; United Archives GmbH/Alamy Stock Photo, p. 42; Jessica Brandi Lifland/Polaris/Newscom, p. 45; © Cmglee/Wikimedia Commons (CC BY-SA 3.0), p. 48; U.S. Air Force photo/Master Sgt. Piper Faulisi, p. 50; © Chip Somodevilla/Getty Images, p. 55; © Mark Wilson/Getty Images, p. 58; NASA, p. 62; © VCG/Getty Images, p. 64; © Jared C. Benedict/Wikimedia Commons (CC BY-SA 2.5), p. 65; © Charles Pertwee/Bloomberg/Getty Images, p. 66; © TORU YAMANAKA/AFP/Getty Images, p. 67; Kyle J. O. Olson/U.S. Marines, p. 68; Frederic Neema/Polaris/Newscom, p. 76; Ssg Matthew B. Fredericks/ZUMA Press/Newscom, p. 80; © Elliott Marks/Paramount/REX/Shutterstock, p. 82; © MGM/Stanley Kubrick Productions/REX/Shutterstock, p. 85; © BSIP/UIG/Getty Images, p. 88; © MANDEL NGAN/AFP/Getty Images, p. 90.

Front cover: © iStockphoto.com/jani001. Back cover: © iStockphoto.com/standret.

About the Author

A former teacher and journalist, Stephanie Sammartino McPherson has written more than thirty books. She especially enjoys writing about science and technology. Her award-winning and star-reviewed books include *Iceberg Right Ahead: The Tragedy of the Titanic*, *Arctic Thaw: Climate Change and the Global Race for Energy Resources*, and *Doping in Sports: Winning at Any Cost?*